COLIN WILSON

INTRODUCTION to the NEW EXISTENTIALISM

HOUGHTON MIFFLIN COMPANY BOSTON

1967

First Printing R

Library of Congress Catalog Card Number: 67-15030
Printed in the United States of America

For Maurice Cranston

CONTENTS

PREFACE

The purpose of this book is described in its title. The philosophy that is at present known as existentialism is identified mainly with the names of Kierkegaard, Heidegger and Sartre. It is fundamentally pessimistic – even nihilistic – and a limit seems to have been reached in its development. For more than twenty-five years, there has been no new contribution; Kierkegaard's *Unscientific Postscript*, Heidegger's *Being and Time* and Sartre's *Being and Nothingness* remain standard works that have not been superseded. Existentialism has halted in a *cul de sac*.

In the six volumes of my 'Outsider sequence',[1] I have attempted to outline a 'new existentialism' that will possess what is so notably lacking in Heidegger and Sartre – the possibility of future development. The present book is an attempt to present the basic arguments of the 'Outsider sequence' in a simple and non-technical language for the ordinary intelligent reader. It presupposes no previous acquaintance with existentialism or with the 'Outsider sequence.' I have preferred to speak of a 'new existentialism' rather than a 'phenomenological existentialism' because it is less of a mouthful; but later in the present volume, the two terms are used as interchangeable.

1. *The Outsider*, 1956, *Religion and the Rebel*, 1957, *The Age of Defeat* (called in America *The Stature of Man*), 1959. *The Strength to Dream*, 1962, *Origins of the Sexual Impulse*, 1963, *Beyond the Outsider*, 1965.

Part One

THE CRISIS IN MODERN THOUGHT

INTRODUCTORY

MY OWN APPROACH TO THE PROBLEM

It is necessary to begin with a definition of existentialism. It is, then, a philosophy that asks the kind of questions that were once regarded as 'religious': questions about the meaning of human existence, freedom and the existence of God.

Modern philosophy was founded by Descartes, who was a scientist and mathematician. It was he who insisted that philosophy should be no more and no less than a science. But Descartes was also a good Catholic, who had no intention of opposing the Church; he therefore kept his philosophy and his religion in different compartments. He accepted that only the Church can provide the answers to questions about the meaning of human existence and human freedom. This meant that what Descartes called philosophy was a matter of 'scientific' questions: What do I mean when I say a statement is 'true'? What is the relation between the mind and the physical world? What is the relation between consciousness and the senses?

For the next two centuries, the mainstream of philosophy accepted the Cartesian tradition that philosophy and religion should be kept in separate compartments. But since religion, in any case, no longer received universal acceptance, this often meant simply that philosophers regarded religious questions as meaningless. This is the view held today by most philosophers of the school of linguistic analysis – which is at present one of the two most influential philosophical movements in the western world. The other is existentialism.

Existentialists do not accept the view that philosophy has no right to ask 'religious' questions. This is not to say that they reject Descartes' idea that philosophy should be a science. But they cannot agree that questions about the 'nature and destiny of man' are meaningless to a scientist, and that therefore it is a waste of time to ask them.

But the question with which I, as an existentialist, have been concerned, is not whether philosophy has a right to ask questions about the meaning of human existence: this I take for granted. There are other assumptions that seem to be made in every book on existentialism with which I cannot agree. It seems to be generally accepted that existentialism is necessarily a philosophy of pessimism – or at least, of a very limited, stoical kind of optimism. Anyone who opens any one of the many books on the subject becomes immediately aware of a certain atmosphere of gloom. In Helmut Kuhn's *Encounter with Nothingness*, for example, the chapter headings give us an immediate sense of this negative content: 'Nothingness Astir,' 'Estrangement,' 'Condemned to be Free,' 'Illumination through Anguish.' One comes to accept sentences like this: 'The struggle through the slough of despondency is conceived as the first phase of a dialectical movement.'

All the existentialist texts that I know – whether by Sartre or Marcel, Jaspers or Camus – seem to share this atmosphere. It is an atmosphere we encounter a great deal in modern literature, even in writers who could not be described as existentialists – Aldous Huxley and Graham

Greene, Samuel Beckett and Eugene Ionesco, Ernest Hemingway and T. S. Eliot. It is completely unlike the atmosphere we encounter in Wells or Shaw or Chesterton, whose presuppositions are optimistic.

But then, the presuppositions of a poet or novelist are personal and emotional; they may be due to his upbringing, or even to his glands. What business have such presuppositions in philosophy?

Let me expand this. Some years ago, an American psychologist, Abraham Maslow, felt the same kind of instinctive revolt against the 'atmosphere' of Freudian psychology, with its emphasis on sickness and neurosis, and decided that he might obtain some equally interesting results if he studied *extremely healthy* people. He therefore looked around for the most cheerful and well-adjusted people he could find, and asked for their co-operation in his studies. He soon discovered an interesting fact: that most extremely healthy people frequently experience moods of intense affirmation and certainty; Maslow called these 'peak experiences.' No one had made this discovery before because it had never struck anyone that a science calling itself 'psychology,' and professing to be a science of the human mind (*not* merely the sick mind), ought to form its estimate of human beings by taking into account healthy minds as well as sick ones. A sick man talks obsessively about his illness; a healthy man never talks about his health; for, as Pirandello points out, we take happiness for granted, and only begin to question life when we are unhappy. Hence no psychologist had ever made this simple and obvious discovery about peak experiences.

The 'peak experience' is not necessarily a mystical experience, although mystical experiences are one form of peak experience. A young mother watching her husband

and children eat breakfast had a 'peak experience'; a hostess sitting alone in the room after a highly successful party had a 'peak experience.' It is a sense of life-affirmation of the kind that Proust described in *Swann's Way*, when he wrote, 'I had ceased now to feel mediocre, accidental, mortal. . . .'

The interesting word here is 'accidental.' For Sartre, the most basic characteristic of the human situation is what he calls 'contingency,' man's sense that he is somehow not 'necessary,' that he is an accident. The suicide is, in fact, making a practical affirmation of this notion. Sartre, Camus and Heidegger take man's 'contingency' to be a basic fact of human existence; man must recognise that he is not the object of a constant loving attention of God or Providence; in the universal sense, he is insignificant. If we look through photographs of suicides in a volume on forensic medicine, this sense of man's contingency strikes us like a blow; the disfigured corpse seems to negate every human aspiration, and we are aware that the act of suicide sprang from a sense of the meaninglessness of life, or its pointless horror and cruelty. Heidegger or Sartre, examining such a photograph, would say sadly: 'It is horrible, but it is true; we must face it.'

The peak experience seems to be a denial of man's *contingency*, a sudden insight into *meaning*, when the suicide's negation is seen to be an unfortunate mistake, like a bankrupt who commits suicide a minute before the arrival of a telegram announcing that he has been left a million pounds.

Now the peak experiences described by certain mystics – Pascal, for example – or conveyed on canvas by Van Gogh in his painting of the Starry Night, may be regarded as dubious testimony; a psychologist would point out that both Van Gogh and Pascal were sick. Science makes allowance for the exceptions, but it builds its edifice upon the rules. But if Maslow is right, peak experiences – that deny that life is accidental and meaningless – may no longer be regarded as the exception; we can no longer dismiss them by referring to them as 'abnormal.' Modern literature and psychology play a considerable part in forming the picture that we have of ourselves; but according to Maslow they have been guilty of an under-estimation of man's character and potentialities.

In the present volume, I am concerned to show how the existentialist picture of man – as presented by Sartre or Heidegger or Camus – errs greatly on the side of pessimism, and to show how this error has arisen. What is usually meant by existentialism – the philosophy that began with Kierkegaard and is today represented by Sartre, Marcel and the rest – is consequently no longer a 'living philosophy'; it is as dead as the phlogiston theory of combustion or Hamilton's quaternions. It has run itself into a *cul de sac*, and there is no chance of further development. It was obvious that Camus had reached an impasse some years before his death. Heidegger's thought has been static for at least thirty-five years. Sartre's attempt to wriggle his neck out of the noose of his own pessimism, in the *Critique of Dialectical Reason*, is a failure; he remains awkwardly suspended between philosophical nihilism and Marxian optimism[1].

1. In fact, of course, Sartre's *Critique* is not an attempt to advance his existentialism a stage further; it is merely an attempt to create a 'working compromise' with Marxism. Admittedly, as Maurice Cranston has pointed out, it is Marxism that is expected to make all the concessions. Still, if one does not accept Sartre's basic premise – that Marxism is the most important modern philosophy, of which we are all forced to take notice – then there is no point in reading the book.

But this is not to say that existentialism is dead: only that in its Kierkegaard-Sartre form it has reached a point from which it can neither advance nor retreat. I shall refer to this Kierkegaard-Sartre form as the 'old existentialism' or simply as existentialism. My purpose is to outline a new form of existentialism that avoids this *cul de sac*, and that can continue to develop. It rejects Sartre's notion of man's contingency – for reasons which I shall discuss in detail. Its bias is therefore distinctly optimistic, and its atmosphere is as different from that of the 'old existentialism' as the atmosphere of G. K. Chesterton's novels differ from *Waiting for Godot*. Its methods might be described as Anglo-Saxon and empirical rather than as 'continental' and metaphysical. This might seem to be a betrayal of the whole existentialist outlook; but it should be remembered that Edmund Husserl – in some ways the father-figure of modern existentialism – used to tell his students that they could learn more from David Hume than from any other philosopher.

CHAPTER ONE

THE OLD EXISTENTIALISM

The destruction of Meaning–
Kierkegaard–Karl Jaspers–Martin Heidegger–Sartre–Camus–
Why Existentialism is a failure

Existentialism is a humanism: that is to say, it could never have come into being in an age of religious faith. It is a post-Christian philosophy. Mediaeval man believed that life was meaningful because God had created man, and Christ had redeemed him; this was the meaning of life. Although Søren Kierkegaard regarded himself as a Christian, he belonged to an age that could no longer feel comfortable in the 'bosom of God.' Kierkegaard's starting point is the feeling that life is a question mark. He wanted to pass beyond interrogation into faith; but it is clear from his work that he never succeeded.

Nineteenth-century man felt as if he had been thrown out of the Garden of Eden; he was in the world on his own. He might, with great difficulty, find his way back to some faith and affirmation; but the old sense of peace and universal order had vanished.

It is a commonplace to say that this had happened because of the rise of science; but this is only a half-truth. The real reason was that science suddenly became a way of thought, a way of life. It had never been this for Sir Isaac Newton. For Newton, science was a game, like chess. He was an enthusiastic player – but the source of his emotional life, his sense of meaning, lay in religion; he regarded his commentary on the Book of Daniel as far more important than the *Principia* or the infinitesimal calculus. It is true that Newton was inclined to mix religion with his science – he endorsed Plato's remark that God geometrises – but he was less inclined to rationalise his religion than to religionise his science. Like all great men, he had a thirst for *meaning*; and it was religion that satisfied this thirst, not science. He would have been horrified by the modern universe of science.

Newton's successors lacked the religious temperament; besides, they were intoxicated with the possibilities of science. By the mid-nineteenth century, the scientific revolution was complete; but in its old form – of dogma and absolute authority – there were few intelligent men who could endorse it.

This was the situation when existentialism appeared on the scene. Kierkegaard was the first to use the word, but the credit might more fairly be given to J. G. Hamann, a contemporary and opponent of Kant, or to William Blake, or even to Blaise Pascal. These were all men of a strongly sceptical and rational turn of mind, but possessed of a thirst for *meaning* that science was not strong enough to satisfy. A few centuries earlier, they might have been labelled unbelievers and burnt; but in the Age of Reason, they found themselves in the paradoxical position of asserting that man has needs that are not satisfiable by reason alone.

Looking at the matter today, it is impossible to support one side or the other. History, as usual, was achieving progress by a series of violent swings from one side to the other, each one of which went too far. The Greeks produced a galaxy of good-natured gods; the Jews countered with a single jealous God. Christianity modified Him to a somewhat bad-tempered but fundamentally benevolent deity, to whom man owes absolute allegiance. Science pointed out that Christianity consists largely of dogmas and lies, and scrapped the lot. Blake and Kierkegaard pointed out that even if religion is ninety-nine per cent nonsense, it is the one per cent of truth that counts, and wasted their energies on diatribes against science and reason. It can be seen that the history of ideas seems to be pursuing the zig-zag course of a drunkard.

Kierkegaard

Kierkegaard, then, must be understood largely as a philosopher in revolt. Most revolutionaries look old-fashioned to the following century. If this is not true of Kierkegaard, it is only because it has taken us so long to see through the fallacies of nineteenth-century science. But in fact, most of what Kierkegaard had to say is irrelevant to the twentieth century; he was a brilliant neurotic, dying of frustration and stagnation in a provincial city. Compared to William Blake, he was not even a particularly bold thinker. Blake was concerned with 'peak experiences'; he opposed science for the same reason that science opposed mediaeval religion: because he felt it turned man into a worm. Kierkegaard also declared that the reality of the human situation is too complex for science to grasp; but he was no optimistic visionary; on the contrary, he took a perverse pleasure in reviving a narrow, Jewish form of dogmatism. The harshness of the Old Testament struck him as a pleasing alternative to the stupidities of Copenhagen society, so he misused his brilliance in defending it. The story of the sacrifice of Isaac was re-interpreted in terms of a subtle modern psychology, and became a parable of 'the appalling strangeness of the mercy of God.'

But the absurdities and excesses of Kierkegaard's philosophy are less important than the urge behind them, the agonised thirst for meaning that was only partly the result of neurotic maladjustment and sexual frustration. It is this thirst for meaning that makes Kierkegaard relevant to our own time.

There is no space here to try to trace in detail the complicated history of existentialism since Kierkegaard; it would involve an account of the ideas of Nietzsche, Bergson, Lachelier, Dilthey, Scheler, Jaspers, Heidegger, Camus, Sartre and Marcel, as well as numerous digressions on idealism, realism and pragmatism. Unfortunately, in spite of this impressive list of names, there has been little real advance beyond Kierkegaard's rather negative position. For practical purposes, it will be enough to speak briefly of Jaspers, Heidegger and Sartre.

Karl Jaspers

Jaspers (born 1883) began as a clinical psychologist, working in a mental hospital in Heidelberg. This led him to produce his first major work, his *Psychopathology*, an attempt at a comprehensive description of all mental illness. Jaspers did not write as a Freudian, or a member of any specific school. And it was this freedom from theoretical preconception that led him into philosophy. He saw that the idea of mental illness presupposes the idea of 'normality.' Normality can be defined in two ways: either in terms of dogmatic religion, where man's purpose and function are clearly defined, or in terms of materialistic science, which considers man purely as a social animal. Jaspers, in fact, was facing the same problem as Kierkegaard. He attacked the problem with German thoroughness, writing a thousand-page history of philosophy attempting to show how the problem has arisen. (At the time of writing – 1965 – he is engaged on another similar enterprise called *The Great Philosophers*, whose first volume alone is 968 pages long.) This has led him to results that are singularly difficult to define, except in terms of negatives. Man makes the mistake of regarding knowledge as something concrete, which applies to his reality as a historical being. But when a philosopher becomes really absorbed in the history of his subject, he sees that knowledge is only the movement of man's spirit towards Transcendence. The various forms of knowledge become prisons for the human spirit – as Christianity became a great dogma – but man can only be free if he can grasp that it is he who creates the dogma. This is the point of huge enterprises like *Philosophy* and *The Great Philosophers*: to encourage the human mind to grasp its place in the great forward movement of the spirit. Forms of knowledge are a 'cypher-script of Being,' and the philosopher aims at reading the script behind the temporary forms.

This does not sound very clear; the reason, perhaps, is that Jaspers is not very clear either. Unlike Camus or Sartre, he cannot be easily summarised; his thought moves in great sweeps, and his meanings only begin to emerge after one has read a hundred pages or so. But what *is* clear is the pessimistic tone of his thought. Man encounters his true self only in the boundary situations of existence – death, suffering, guilt, the sudden violent accident.

One feels finally of Jaspers that he has clearly grasped the need for a new kind of philosophy, a new way for man to grasp his knowledge, but he has spent most of his strength in trying to explain how the situation has come about. His thought seems to move on the slippery ground of the existential paradox: that to *live* is the opposite of to know: so human knowledge can never grasp human existence. It must always falsify it. This is the paradox that defeated Kierkegaard. Again and again, as one struggles with Jaspers' difficult terminology, one feels that he is on the point of giving up, because words and ideas are so inadequate for conveying the living, complicated stuff of human existence. If a philosopher's importance depends upon his advancing his subject to a new stage – and to handing on vital results to his successors – then Jaspers must be judged a failure.

Martin Heidegger

By this criterion, the same must be said of Martin Heidegger. The first thing that must be understood about Heidegger is that his temperament is close to that of Kierkegaard and Pascal; he is a poet and something of a mystic. In reading Heidegger, one is constantly aware of his rejection of 'the herd.' Jaspers' basic obsession is the great sweep of all human thought; Heidegger's is the poet, standing apart from society, and receiving sudden flashes of insight into the true nature of human existence. He can never communicate these insights to the herd because of the very nature of a herd – its tendency to look around continually at the rest of the herd, to live in other people's eyes, And yet paradoxically, the driving force behind civilisation is the vital impulse of the men who stand alone.

Because of this feeling of the immense difficulty of saying anything important, Heidegger, like Jaspers, makes very heavy weather of the business of communication; in fact, he is the most obscure of modern philosophers.

Nevertheless, his central insight is easy to express. Man is a strange, inauthentic creature who has very little contact with real Existence. Intellectuals cut themselves off from reality by trapping themselves in a world of concepts; ordinary men are cut off from reality because they are so self-absorbed, so involved in the pettiness of everyday existence. They live in a meaningless world because they find it so difficult to *mean* anything. Chesterton pointed out: we say 'Thank you' when someone passes the salt, but we don't mean it; we say the earth is round, but we don't mean it (even though it happens to be true). We are all trapped in a world of dreams inside our own skulls, and nothing short of the threat of immediate death will wake us up to intense appreciation of our lives. We have forgotten that the world out there *really exists*. For most of us, it is a shadow world. Improved techniques of communication have only blurred the outlines further; we live so much through books, films, television, etc., that dream and reality have only become further confused.

This is the trouble – 'forgetfulness of Existence.' The problem is somehow to get back to Existence. In *The Doors of Perception*, Aldous Huxley said that a dose of mescalin suddenly made him aware of a chair as a blazing atom of existence – the chair almost became *alive* with existence, like the chair painted by Van Gogh of which Gauguin said, 'No one ever painted a chair like that before.' This is what we have forgotten – and what poets never entirely forget. They are always being startled by the sheer beauty and alienness of the world. For the rest of us, a chair does not really exist; it is little more than a name – a name that means something to support us when we sit down.

This is the problem; but what is to be done about it? Like Jaspers, Heidegger does not seem to be very sure. He devotes a great deal of analysis to the inauthenticity of the herd, the banality of everyday existence. Here he is close to Pascal on the subject of man's needs for amusement and distraction to forget his own emptiness. He recognises that man often springs into 'authentic existence' when confronted with death, and that poets often become aware of it without this stimulus. But beyond this, Heidegger has little that is positive to say. He outlined the problem exhaustively in *Being and Time* in 1927, and has since devoted several short books (which are little more than essays) to discussing the poet – Hölderlin in particular. But as with Kierkegaard, we feel that Heidegger is important because of something he *felt* rather than anything he thought. The drive behind his work is the same hunger for meaning, which he identifies with existence. One might read a great deal of Heidegger – and of books about him – without getting further than this. For the form under which Heidegger presents his problems often sounds nonsensical. For example, he asks: 'Why do things exist rather than not exist?' or 'Why is there something rather than nothing?' This sounds like a question for a theologian or a mystic, not a philosopher; but Heidegger is only trying to draw attention to the reality of existence behind our words. In the same way, he tries to use language in an oddly stilted, clumsy way to try to free the reader's mind of this tendency to associate false or ready-made concepts with his words. The effect is not unlike Hemingway's attempt to make the speech in *For Whom the Bell Tolls* sound like a foreign language by translating literally from the Spanish (or trying to make it sound as if it is). Whether it achieves its effect is a question for philosophers who can read Heidegger in German.

Sartre

For purposes of exposition, Sartre remains the best representative of the modern existentialist tradition.

All its problems and its faults can be seen most clearly in his work. His work also makes it plain why existentialism has advanced so little after Kierkegaard.

The first thing to note about Sartre is that his temperament is naturally gloomy and pessimistic. He is the opposite of what Heidegger means by a poet. Like Heidegger, he is preoccupied by the fact that the world 'exists' quite apart from our minds; but he seems to find this separate existence disquieting – or even nauseating. His novel *Nausea* concerns a historian who has always seen the world in terms of his own intellectual patterns, but who has sudden experiences of 'awakening' when 'things' somehow slip past his intellectual guard; the result is a paralysing sense of nausea. The point worth noting is that this experience is basically the same as the poet's except that the poet suddenly sees reality with a shock of delight. Wordsworth describes rowing on a lake and suddenly receiving a sense of 'other modes of being' from the outline of a mountain in the darkness. For Sartre, the alien modes of being are not a source of hope or pleasure but of nervousness; he feels threatened by them. As we read Sartre's novels, it is clear that he does not like the real world; it always disgusts him slightly, and he usually describes it with adjectives like 'sticky,' 'slimy,' 'oily,' 'nauseating.' His autobiography *Words*, describing his childhood, has none of the usual delight or magic of accounts of childhood. When he describes the sexual act, in *Intimacy* or *Childhood of a Leader*, it is always disappointing or disgusting; there is none of the Lawrence vision of sex as a redeeming force. Again, in *Words*, he writes: '. . . the boat seemed to have detached itself from the lake, and in a moment would be gliding above that rippling swamp' (p. 158). Why is a lake, for Sartre, a 'rippling swamp'? The description is not even accurate;

it simply expresses Sartre's feeling of horror and distrust at the idea of a depth of alien water.

It is to be expected, then, that Sartre's account of the human situation will be devoid of the natural poetry and delight that most of us feel at least once in a while – in short, of 'peak experiences.'

Sartre is as much preoccupied as Heidegger with man's inauthenticity as a social being, with the banality and mediocrity of life lived in the eyes of other people. His dictum 'Hell is other people' is the obverse side of Heidegger's observations about the poet and solitude. But here the interesting problem arises. Since Sartre is so much a stranger to 'peak experiences,' solitude is not really an answer to the problem of the hell of other people. This means that both entrances are blocked. He agrees heartily with Dostoevsky that it is impossible to love your fellow man if you have to have much contact with him; but solitude is no answer; it is likely to lead to nausea, when you realise that hell is other *things* as well as other people.

This problem emerges clearly in Sartre's most important play *Lucifer and the Lord*. The scene is set in the sixteenth century; the hero, Goetz, is a soldier who, as the play opens, is about to invade a town and massacre the inhabitants. Someone remarks that anybody can be evil; in fact, no man has ever succeeded in being good. Goetz takes up the challenge and sets out to become a saint; he becomes the champion of the poor, gives away his lands, and sets up a 'City of the Sun.' But he finds it very difficult to be a good man in a world of fools. When the City of the Sun is finally destroyed by peasants in revolt, Goetz comes to the conclusion that there is no God in the sky, and so it is pointless to try to be a saint. One should live for one's fellow men. He becomes the leader of the peasants' revolt, and stabs an officer who refuses to obey him, remarking that a man may have to serve his fellow men by committing evil as well as good.

What is interesting here is Sartre's strangely negative conception of goodness or saintliness. A saint is a man who behaves in a saintly manner and kisses lepers. (The leper submits wearily, and says he wishes good people would find some other way of advertising their virtue.) It never seems to strike Sartre that a saint may be driven by as powerful an inner-compulsion as a revolutionary or a philosopher, and that his goodness may be only a by-product of some inner evolution. It is clear that Goetz gets no special pleasure from doing evil – sacking cities and raping women; it is merely an assertion of his will. He decides to be good to demonstrate his versatility; it is another assertion of will. Naturally, it leads to nothing.

The point, of course, that Sartre is temperamentally incapable of appreciating, is that the saint's aim is the 'peak experience.' There are no 'peak experiences' in Sartre's world; consequently, both good and evil appear to him to be negative. But in that case, what is left? There is only the negative ideal of doing good to one's fellow men out of lack of anything better to do.

Sartre's philosophy, then, falls into two parts. In his work up to 1950 (the year he wrote *Lucifer and the Lord*) he is concerned with attacking false notions – man's ways of lying to himself, the way he imposes his false concepts on existence, the way he shirks his freedom by pretending he is a mere creature of God. Since 1950, he has tried to take a less negative stand, and has identified himself with the 'working-class movement.' The obvious objection to this latter is that it is not really an answer to the problems propounded by Kierkegaard and Heidegger. One may be an ardent communist, and still recognise that when world communism has been achieved, the philosophical problems – of man's freedom, his relation to existence, etc. – will still be unsolved. Sartre's *Critique of Dialectical Reason* is not a continuation of the work he began in *Being and Nothingness*, but an abandonment of it. One can understand perfectly how he came to write the following passage at the end of *Words*:

'My retrospective illusions are all in pieces. Martyrdom, salvation, immortality: all are crumbling; the building is falling in ruins. I have caught the Holy Ghost in the cellars and flung him out of them. Atheism is a cruel, long-term business: I believe I have gone through it to the end. I see clearly, I am free from illusions . . . for about ten years, I have been a man who is waking up, cured of a long, bitter-sweet madness, who cannot recall his old ways without laughing, *and who no longer has any idea what to do with his life* (my italics). I have become once again the traveller without a ticket that I was at seven . . .

'I have renounced my vocation, but I have not unfrocked myself. I still write. What else can I do?'

What else, since he had been trapped since the age of thirty in the Heidegger paradox, and had never managed to wriggle free? Man, says Heidegger, has forgotten Existence; he must somehow get back to it. Sartre took mescalin when he was twenty-eight, but it produced a state of amplified neurosis; reality became something that leered and threatened. To master reality, one must be detached from it; but from now on, this necessary detachment would strike Sartre as a form of 'bad faith,' of running away. In Heidegger's form, existentialism can still be optimistic. Man deliberately detaches himself to overcome reality, turning it into an abstraction, a mere instrument of his will; then, through poetry or meditation on death, he again 'returns to existence' and is revitalised;

he gets the best of both worlds. For Sartre, there could be no escape; the choice was between the inauthenticity of people and the nausea of things.

Albert Camus

It should here be noted that Sartre's friend and colleague Camus found himself in the same predicament, so that his work had reached a standstill some time before his death in a car accident in 1960. His first novel *The Outsider* is on the familiar Heidegger theme of a man who has totally forgotten existence, and to whom life has consequently become unreal, meaningless. He drifts on from day to day, and even the death of his mother leaves him indifferent. Only the prospect of death at the end of the novel (when he is about to be executed for killing an Arab) breaks the enchantment and brings about the 'return to Existence.'

In *The Myth of Sisyphus* – written at the same time as the novel – Camus recognises that if life is so meaningless, then man's basic problem is whether to commit suicide. Camus then chose the same dubious solution as Sartre – escape from the 'emptiness of the heavens' in the communion of men, the obsession with social justice. (*The Plague*, 1947, *The Rebel*, 1952.)

Now Camus, to some extent, shared Sartre's presupposition about the world of things. The world is imbued with a malicious 'absurdity'; it is not merely indifferent to men but actively hostile. (Camus' outlook in this respect bears some resemblance to that of Thomas Hardy.) This is the theme of *The Outsider*, *The Plague* and the play *Cross Purposes*. He is obsessed by death and the indifference of nature. A highly unpleasant passage in *The Plague* describing the death of a child illustrates what he meant by his 'quarrel with God.'

But the oddest thing about Camus is that he was not a natural born pessimist, like Sartre; it would certainly not be true to say of him (as of Sartre) that he was the opposite of a poet. There are, in fact, several 'peak experiences' in his work – one is described at the end of *The Outsider*, another in a story called *The Woman Taken in Adultery* (which is almost Lawrencian), another in *Les Noces* (a volume of essays). Yet Camus failed to see that these 'peak experiences' might contain the seed of escape from his pessimistic *cul de sac*. (In fact, when the present writer brought up this subject in conversation with him in 1959, he explained that he could not attribute any wide significance to such experiences because they were abnormal, while his philosophy was an attempt to provide a creed for the ordinary man in the modern world.)

In retrospect, it seems that Camus was an overrated writer who was too concerned with effects. There is something artificial, melodramatic, in *The Outsider*, where the hero is hanged because of misunderstanding. One often has this same sense of writing for effect in reading his critical works; they are a little too self-consciously stylish, like an actor who cannot resist showing off a beautiful voice. All this points to the somewhat harsh conclusion that he failed to escape his *cul de sac* because he never tried hard enough to do so.

Why Existentialism is a failure

To summarise: existentialism was a philosophy of man without an organised religion. This is not to say a philosophy of man without God. Many existentialists have believed in God. But there could be no comforting *intermediary* or saviour. Man stood alone. If God existed, then the lonely individual had to find him without help. It all started with romanticism: with Goethe's *Faust* and

Schiller's *Robbers* and Shelley's *Prometheus Unbound*, with men demanding why they should be mere creatures. If the church was an imposture and the scriptures merely inspired poetry, then the individual suddenly had a new freedom and a new dignity thrust upon him. In fact, as Dostoevsky saw quite clearly, man himself must become God – or a god. The romantics found this burden too heavy; it was thrust upon them too suddenly after the comfort and stability of the 18th century. They were being asked to grow up too quickly. Many committed suicide or died of various illnesses, and by the end of the century, the Byronic spirit of God-defiance had become a mood of heavy nostalgia and defeat. Kierkegaard and Nietzsche were as much romantics as existentialists; but Jaspers, Heidegger, Sartre, Camus and the rest wrote as thinkers rather than as poets. With them, existentialism became an intellectualised romanticism. It had a tougher quality than its nineteenth-century predecessor, and instead of ending in nostalgia and defeat, it has ended in stoicism and defeat.

Existentialism, like romanticism, is a philosophy of freedom. It has reached a standstill because no existential thinker can agree that there are any values outside man – that is, outside man's ordinary, everyday consciousness. Man is free, says Sartre. But what is he to do with his freedom? He can do anything he likes, Sartre replies. But then, just as everybody's business is nobody's business, so freedom for anything is freedom for nothing. Man is free, but the world is empty and meaningless – this is the problem. While this sentence remains a summary of existentialism, there is nothing further to be done.

CHAPTER TWO

WHAT IS PHENOMENOLOGY?

Why Phenomenology became necessary–God the Confidence Trickster–Husserl's Solution—the detective and the suspects–Intentionality—the basic concept of Phenomenology–Crabbe's Lover's Journey

There is a chapter in the history of existentialism to which I have not so far referred, although it is of crucial importance. In fact, it provides the way out of the *cul de sac.* I am referring to the philosophical method founded by Husserl, and known as phenomenology.

There is an initial difficulty here. The literature on existentialism is considerable, ranging from highly technical works to popular expositions. Twenty years ago, many of the important texts were in foreign languages; now this can no longer be said. In comparison, the phenomenological movement has been badly served. Important works of Husserl and Merleau-Ponty have been translated into English, but these are certainly not to be recommended to the beginner. As to 'popular expositions,' there are, as far as I know, none in any language. Even a brilliant and straightforward text like Maurice Natanson's *Literature, Philosophy and the Social Sciences* depends on the reader possessing a certain basic acquaintance with the ideas and methods of Husserl.

In the present book, I shall therefore attempt to provide a simple and clear outline of the aims of phenomenology.

Why Phenomenology became necessary – God the Confidence Trickster

Descartes proposed that philosophy should be a science. One should begin, he said, by doubting everything; one should *take nothing for granted*. After all, it seems perfectly obvious that the sun goes round the earth; yet it is not true. Now supposing (for the sake of argument) that God was a confidence trickster, a magician whose aim was to completely deceive us. Would man have any hope of ever arriving at the truth? At first sight, no, for surely God holds all the cards? On second thoughts it is not quite so hopeless. There are certain things that even God cannot do; for example, he cannot un-happen something after it has happened. And if I watch a conjuror closely, I may not be able to decide how he does his tricks, but at least my reason can make *some* progress. For example, the rabbit was either already in the hat – hidden in the lining, perhaps – or it was concealed in the conjuror's sleeve.

So Descartes proposed that if man doubts everything, he is bound to arrive at a residue of truth that is undoubtable. This will become the foundation of philosophy. Descartes managed to doubt a great deal that is generally taken for granted. For example, he saw a robot in the king's garden, and this led him to ask how he could know for certain that men are not simply robots. This question almost brought his philosophising to a halt. For obviously, *if* God were a confidence trickster, he could be deceiving Descartes that the world is full of other men like himself when it is really full of robots. In that case, where was the point of philosophy? Descartes hastily pushed aside this possibility, deciding that it is not common sense. But he *did* accept that animals are probably robots. He reasoned that he could be sure that *he* was not a robot (I think, therefore I am), and that he would simply have to take it on trust that other men are also alive.

But Descartes had introduced a dangerous method. Bishop Berkeley proceeded to 'doubt everything,' and concluded that if God is a confidence trickster, then perhaps the world is an illusion which only exists as long as I am looking at it. After all, I only know the world through my senses, and my senses vary from day to day; if I have a bad hangover, for example, my food will taste like sawdust. Supposing that my senses are not merely fickle: supposing they are downright liars, in league with God to convince us that the world exists when it really doesn't?

Hume took this argument a step further. If I put a kettle on the fire, I assume that it will get hotter. But supposing this is yet another trick? Supposing it ought really to freeze, but God makes it boil to deceive us? Supposing, in fact, that *cause and effect* are another confidence trick, and effects do not really follow causes at all?

Kant went one stage further (although this seems impossible). Surely $1 + 1 = 2$ is an example of cause and effect? In that case, perhaps one and one really equals three? Hume might argue that $1 + 1 = 2$ is not cause and effect. If I have one apple and I add another, two is not something separate from one and one: it is *the same thing* – whereas a cold kettle is not at all the same thing as a hot kettle. Kant, however, would not have this. Addition is cause and effect, he said, and then went on to add that, in fact, *everything* is in the mind. Not merely colours and shapes and tastes (which vary according to our senses) but mathematics and space and time as well.

Kant's aim in proposing this vertiginous solution was not – as might be supposed – to make nonsense of all philosophy, but to try to save religion. The first victim of Descartes' 'radical doubt' was the Bible and the church, followed by all morality. The rationalists pointed out that, if it is a question of certainty, religion falls a long way behind science. Kant reversed the argument; if *everything* was in the mind, then science is just as doubtful as religion – which is to say that religion is as certain as science. It is difficult nowadays for us to understand how this absurdity ever imposed upon anyone; but it must be remembered that, at the time, it seems a rigorous and logical deduction from Descartes' unshakable premises.

Philosophy after Kant became a tower of Babel – but Descartes remained the foundation. Some thinkers followed his materialist line. Perhaps man *is* a robot? Perhaps the fact that I think does not prove that I really exist – after all, a robot might think, and imagine it possessed a living soul? Others pursued the 'idealist' line from Descartes through Kant; this culminated in Hegel's vision of all history as a great movement of the spirit – an idea that Jaspers arrived at by a different route. But the trouble with both materialism and idealism was that they both seemed to be dead-ends.

Husserl's Solution – the detective and the suspects

This was the situation when Husserl came on the scene at the beginning of the present century. It was Husserl who pointed out the simple mistake that had kept philosophy at a standstill for two hundred years. Descartes had said that man cannot be certain of anything except his own consciousness, and that therefore philosophy should begin with a study of consciousness; but this was the very thing that Descartes neglected to do. He thought of his consciousness as a mirror reflecting the world. He agreed that the mirror might be *distorting* the world; but he replied that man can never have any way of knowing whether this is true. His soul can never get 'out there,' into the outside world; it has to sit inside his head, looking out through his eyes. It never struck him that *the mirror itself might be a variable.*

It is fitting that Husserl should have been an almost exact contemporary of Freud. For it was Freud who had first brought the concept of the unconscious mind to the forefront of psychology. Freud suggested, for example, that a man who left his umbrella behind might actually want to return to the house, and so have subconsciously willed himself to forget it. That is to say, the oversight was *intentional*, yet not consciously so.

Now Husserl was not – as far as is known – at all influenced by Freud; but his suggestion was in the Freudian spirit. The philosopher says that his aim is to understand the universe, and he does this by peering out through the windows of the senses and asking questions. But he is assuming that there are no questions to be asked about his own mind; he takes it for granted that it is a mirror reflecting reality; so that when Descartes says 'I,' he means 'I' – René Descartes, a simple unity, which knows all about itself, and need ask no further questions. It is rather as if a detective is questioning a roomful of suspects, any one of whom might have committed the murder. Unfortunately, the detective was not present at the time of the murder, so he has no 'direct evidence' to go on; he dare not make any assumptions about who is innocent or guilty; he must begin by doubting everything that everyone tells him, and simply use his own enquiring mind to add up the various stories, to perceive contradictions, to weigh the evidence. This is the Cartesian picture of the philosopher. Now Husserl has suggested a new and most disturbing possibility. *Suppose the detective himself is the murderer* – ? The detective begins by assuring himself that he will make no assumptions about who is guilty, that he will doubt everything; but he *has* made an assumption – about *his own innocence*. But philosophers ever since Descartes have been making the same assumption, and philosophy has always found itself in the same *cul de sac*.

This, in essence, is Husserl's message: philosophy wishes to be a science, and it consequently sets out to study the universe scientifically – that is, to ask questions and make observations. But philosophy is not a science while it fails to recognise that there is an equally large area for study *inside man himself*. Consciousness must not be taken for granted as something too obvious to need further questioning. Consciousness itself must be studied. After all, psychology is also a science – the study of that which is inside man. While philosophy confines itself to the external universe, it is only half a science. And it is possibly because it is only half a science that it finds itself at a standstill.

This leads Husserl to define phenomenology as 'the study of the structure of consciousness.' The word 'structure' may give some difficulty at first; after all, structure usually refers to buildings. But then, in Freud's view, the mind is a kind of building, with the unconscious mind as its cellar (while some students of extra-sensory perception suggest that it also has an attic – a kind of super-consciousness – which is also beyond our everyday consciousness). Husserl uses the word 'consciousness' for the whole mind, but apart from this, his view is not fundamentally unlike Freud's.

Intentionality – the basic concept of Phenomenology

But the central concept of phenomenology, and the seed from which it grew, is the notion of intentionality. I have said that Freud explains the leaving behind of an umbrella as 'intentional,' and this conveys the essence of what is meant by the idea. But how can this kind of intentionality make any difference to the basic problems of philosophy? To make this quite clear will require a somewhat lengthy examination of this important concept. It is the key not only to phenomenology, but to a new existentialism.

Consider, first of all, the following diagram, known to experimental psychologists as the Müller-Lyer illusion:

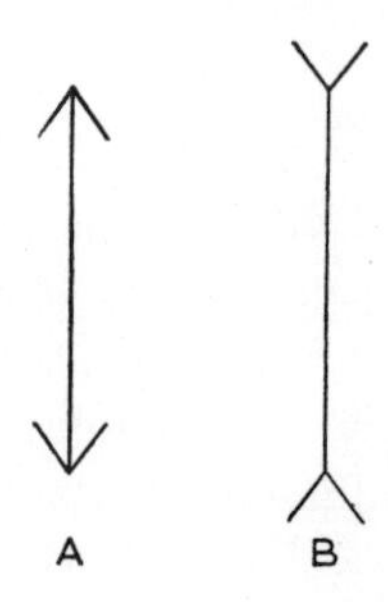

It shows a kind of double-headed arrow, and a double-forked twig. The central lines of the arrow and the twig are of exactly the same length; but the twig appears longer than the arrow because the eye follows the movement of the twig along the forks, while the arrow-heads inhibit this motion of the eye.

By measuring the central lines, one can easily verify that they are the same length. And yet even then, they continue to *appear* to be different lengths. Now this is not an 'emotional prejudice' or disturbance, like leaving the umbrella behind. It is the eye itself that is 'telling lies,' or appears to be doing so. And this is Descartes' 'passive consciousness' that can be trusted to reflect the world faithfully!

Consciousness itself, that is to say, is intentional. It is not a plane mirror, merely reflecting the world. It makes its own distortions, quite apart from our natural human tendency to distort the world through our emotions and prejudices.

Crabbe's Lover's Journey

But let us retrace our steps for a moment, and consider some more obvious examples of intentionality. To begin with, if I put a florin in a cigarette machine and get out a packet of cigarettes, this is clearly *not* intentionality. The machine cannot 'intend' – although, if there is something wrong with its mechanism, it may give two packets of cigarettes, or none at all. Still, this is a defect, not an act of intention.

As I go through an ordinary day, a great many stimuli are dropped into my senses, and I respond to them like a machine. But the same stimuli do not always produce the same response. Here, my attitude of mind makes all the difference.

George Crabbe has a narrative poem called *The Lover's Journey* that would have delighted Husserl. It begins with the thoroughly phenomenological statement:

> 'It is the soul that sees; the outward eyes
> Present the object; but the mind descries.'

The lover sets out to see his mistress, and as he rides along, everything delights him, and his reflections on the delights of nature are of the kind we find in Goldsmith's *Deserted Village* or Thompson's *Seasons*. He passes some gypsies, and reflects charitably that even if they are thieves and idlers, they are nevertheless 'merry rogues.' But when he arrives at her house, he finds a note saying that she has had to go to visit a friend, and asking him to follow. He sets out in a thoroughly black temper; now everything displeases him:

> 'I hate these long green lanes; there's nothing seen
> In this vile country but eternal green.'

The sight of a newly wedded couple emerging from church arouses cynical reflections. But now he arrives and meets his mistress, and instantly forgets his anger. They go off together, completely oblivious of everything but one another. The passing scenes arouse neither delight nor irritation; they are unnoticed.

This is an example of the emotions affecting consciousness. We can observe many other examples every day. The act of falling in love not only reveals the intentionality of the emotions, but is an example of another Husserlian activity – bracketing. A man who is strongly inclined to fall in love finds a girl who suits him; but unless she is completely irresistible, or he completely lacks emotional discipline, he will not find himself falling in love against his will (i.e. automatically). He may first of all find out whether the girl is already married or engaged; if she is not, she becomes a more eligible object of affection. He will also want to know whether she shows any preliminary signs of interest in himself. But even supposing that this is so, he may still find that certain things about her irritate him – a tendency to giggle, a gold tooth, the shape of her nose. But if he is already in the process of falling in love, he will deliberately 'bracket out' these things from his attention, so that he no longer notices them. He may even go further and acquire a taste for them, so that they now give him actual pleasure.

The ordinary physical process of acquiring a taste is also obviously intentional. If I go to a foreign country and am given some strange food or drink, my first reaction may be disappointment. Then, for various reasons, I convince myself that I enjoy it: and, in fact, I *do* come to enjoy it. This may be due to nostalgia for the foreign country, or to a kind of snobbishness – a desire to feel that I have unusual or highly developed tastes – or simply that I get used to it. I shall acquire the taste if acquiring it somehow strikes me as an adventure; I shall refuse to acquire it if it strikes me either as a bore or an inconvenience. But in either case, it is my 'intentionality' that makes all the difference. Chesterton pointed out that an adventure is an inconvenience rightly considered, and that an inconvenience is an adventure wrongly considered.

These are examples of emotional intentionality, and we are all fairly used to this kind of intentionality. There is also physical intentionality, of which we are less aware, because we think of the body as a machine which is hardly subject to our emotions. If I am lying in bed and I cannot get to sleep, my left foot may begin to itch. If I scratch it, the itch transfers to my shoulder blade or my left elbow. At this point, I may recognise that I can make any part of my body itch by simply wondering whether it is itching.

This simple phenomenon is obviously the basis of all psycho-somatic illnesses. The Greek novelist Kanzantzakis, for example, described how he once agreed to meet an attractive woman in her room, but when he woke up in the morning, found that his face had swollen, and a yellow liquid was running from his lower lip. He had been obsessed for a long time by the idea of asceticism; his body was simply interfering to guarantee his chastity. The psychologist Stekel told Kanzantzakis that in the Middle Ages, this was called 'saint's malady' – saints who were tempted to give up their lives in the desert and go to the cities would break out into horrible running sores.

Sex in general forms an interesting subject of study for the phenomenologist because it is partly an emotional and partly a physical activity; and both aspects are subject to 'intentionality.' Again, we are inclined to think of sexual desire as an 'automatic' physical activity, particularly as a sexual stimulus may produce a strong effect as an automatic reflex. Yet the phenomenon of 'le fiasco' shows that a man *carries* his sexual desire towards its object, and may stumble on the way and drop it. Masturbation reveals the completely intentional nature of sexual activity; here the mind simply 'intends' an imaginary sexual object.

Intentionality, then, can exist on many levels. It may be almost conscious – as when I persuade myself that I shall enjoy an experience that is likely to be unpleasant – or completely unconscious, as in the case of the Müller-Lyer effect, and many other similar visual illusions that are used by psychiatrists.

All this is to say that intentionality is applied to acts that we suppose to be *mechanical*, and that we actually cause ourselves. We think something merely 'happens,' like a stone falling when we drop it, when actually we ourselves have caused it to happen.

When intentionality occurs on the conscious or almost-conscious level, Sartre calls it 'bad faith.' A man knows what he is doing – as, for example, when he is giving way to some discreditable impulse – but prefers to turn away from his knowledge because he refuses to make himself uncomfortable. Bad faith, in short, is a kind of spiritual or psychological laziness.

Here are a few more examples of intentionality, chosen at random, to enable the reader to grasp its implications:

(a) If I stare at clouds, I can see various shapes or faces. If I look elsewhere for a moment, the faces will have vanished – not because the clouds have changed, but because I only 'saw' the faces by carefully *adjusting* my attention so as to notice certain things and exclude others.

(b) When my small daughter falls down, I can see her actually making up her mind whether she will cry or not – whether she will allow herself to feel hurt or upset, or whether to get on with the game.

(c) Sometimes one can get drunk on two glasses of beer, and sometimes one can drink whisky for a whole evening and still feel sober. Drunkenness is only partly physical; to a far greater degree, it depends on intentionality.

(d) When I feel sick, I can usually prevent myself from being sick by a certain attitude of mind – a deliberate summoning of my healthy energies. This, of course, applies generally to our physical condition. Headaches are usually a matter of intentionality.

(e) Sleepiness. I may go to bed feeling completely exhausted, unable to fix my attention on anything. If someone roused me because the house next door had caught fire the sleepiness would vanish.

(f) I meet a man I have often seen at a distance – perhaps on stage or television – and I am startled that his face is quite unlike my mental picture of it. I realise that when I saw it at a distance, I only saw certain of its characteristics, and my imagination added the others – mostly by a process of association of ideas, recalling faces that he reminded me of. Yet watching him on television, I could have sworn that I was merely 'seeing' him, and not 'adding' anything at all.

It will now be seen what was meant by the suggestion that 'the detective might be the murderer.' An analogous shift in perspective occurred in modern physics when Einstein, Planck and Heisenberg discovered that the completely passive observer is a fallacy. The universe behaves like a schoolboy trying to write with the teacher looking over his shoulder; it becomes self-conscious, and behaves differently.

Descartes thought that he could discover what the universe was all about by sitting in his armchair and asking questions – just like the scientist – and all subsequent thinkers made the same assumption. Nowadays even scientists know this is wishful thinking. The mind is not a mirror; it is a complicated apparatus made of prisms, mirrors and lenses, and philosophy cannot even begin until it knows the exact nature of the apparatus.

It should be clear now, then, that the word 'intentionality' means in philosophy precisely what it means in everyday life. You may knock over a glass of water accidentally, or intentionally – on purpose.

But it is difficult to grasp the idea of my perceptions being 'intentional'. After all, if I sit on a pin, I do not 'intend' it to hurt me; it just does.

But here it must be understood that the phenomenologist does not deny a non-intentional element in perception. If he did, he would be in the position of Bishop Berkeley or Kant, declaring that the mind creates everything it sees. Phenomenology starts from the recognition that the outside world is 'really there'; my mind does not create it. But then, this page you are reading is also 'really there,' and I have put a certain meaning into its sentences. But if you read it when your attention is wandering, you may read the whole page without grasping anything. No matter how clearly I write, it will mean nothing unless your mind does half the work. What is more, you had to learn to read; and also, since you are reading a book about philosophy, you had to learn to think. There are many people to whom this book would be meaningless no matter how clearly it was written.

Learning to read does not come naturally; we are not born with the ability. Neither does learning to think. On the other hand, we assume that we are born with the ability to see and hear; so we make the mistake of assuming that seeing and hearing simply 'happen' – automatically, not intentionally. This is not so. It is true that we are born already able to see, but this does not mean that it did not have to be learned, like reading. It only means that our distant ancestors did the learning for us, and have managed to pass it on to us genetically. It is just conceivable that at some distant date in the future, babies might be born already able to read their own language – stranger biological mutations have taken place. In that case, some phenomenologist of the future will have difficulty in making them understand that reading is 'intentional,' not something that just 'happens' when the eye falls on written language.

But then, it is not strictly true that we do not have to learn to see. Any painter will tell you that he had to 'learn to see.' And according to Eric Kennington, the Arabs he drew for Lawrence's *Seven Pillars of Wisdom* often completely failed to recognise their portraits. Not only that: they could see nothing on the paper but a mass of confused lines that might have been anything.

All of this may seem interesting enough, but of dubious relevance to the question of a new existentialism. But we now make the leap to a most important point. We 'read' the world around us; it is actually a confused mass of sights and sounds. Our senses filter out about ninety per cent of the sights and sounds so that we do not even have to notice them. (The nerves have small gaps called synapses; strong impulses can jump these gaps like an electric spark, but weak ones are filtered out; otherwise we should be aware of every minute change in the temperature of the room, and wearing a woollen vest would be like wearing barbed wire.) The senses then learn to find their way among the confusion of the remaining ten per cent by inventing convenient formulas and short cuts (like the little rhymes at school that helped us to remember laws of physics or the order of the colours in the spectrum). It sorts the world out into convenient symbols, and attaches more or less importance to various symbols according to its inclination. G. K. Chesterton has an interesting Father Brown story called *The Invisible Man*, in which a murderer manages to get in and out of a house without being seen, although the house is under observation. The murderer turns out to be a postman, and no one has noticed him because a postman is not thought of as a man; he is merely a symbol of a social service. The Chesterton plot is perhaps a little far-fetched, but it points a truth: *to see something really means to notice it, to give significance to it with one's vision.*

But there is a still further point. Through millions of years of evolution, the human eye has succeeded in an apparently impossible feat: in distinguishing between energy with a wavelength of seven hundred thousandths of a centimetre and energy with a wavelength of four hundred thousandths of a centimetre. In fact, it is capable of distinguishing far finer shades of energy, for the two figures I have given are the wavelengths of red and violet light, and the eye can actually distinguish all the colours between the two ends of the spectrum. It does this by a simple and obvious method – by inventing the seven colours of the spectrum, and attaching these to different wavelengths. The eye cannot, at the moment, distinguish any smaller wavelengths than violet – there would be no point, since very few bodies emit energy of such wavelengths; but if it suddenly became necessary for the survival of the human race for the eye to distinguish higher wavelengths than violet, it would simply 'invent' new colours, which do not at present exist.

This problem of colour was one of the things that used to bother scientists who held a strictly materialistic standpoint. We can explain light in mathematical terms – as wavelengths – but we cannot explain the actual difference that the eye sees between two colours; red is quite different from green, and the difference is a difference in *kind*, not in quantity (wavelength). Precisely; and phenomenology makes the strictly materialist standpoint completely untenable. What is essential about human beings and human experience is inexpressible in terms of science; if Descartes had known about wavelengths and had some training in phenomenology, he would not have needed to say 'I think, therefore I am' to prove that man is not a robot; the phenomenon of colour would have proved it far more conclusively.

It will now be seen why phenomenology has an important bearing on existentialism. Philosophy is usually defined as the attempt to understand the universe, and existentialism is concerned with man's relation to the universe. But life is largely a matter of habits – and phenomenological analysis reveals a new depth of meaning in this commonplace assertion – and habit means taking for granted. Science is the opposite of taking for granted. A novelist is entitled to his personal viewpoint; so – to a lesser extent – is a historian; but the scientist attempts to be completely objective, to exclude prejudices and habits of thought from this viewpoint. An existential philosopher cannot even begin to be objective until he knows something about his habits of thought – what he takes for granted because it happens to be the most convenient way of grasping the world. Nietzsche pointed out cynically that most philosophy is little more than a record of the whims and prejudices of philosophers – a kind of disguised autobiography. He was right; this was inevitably so *before Husserl.* A philosopher might be self-critical enough to keep his actual prejudices out of his philosophy; but he still took his perceptions for granted, and regarded his consciousness as a kind of photographic plate that could not lie. Under these circumstances, a philosophy called existentialism – and devoted to understanding the human condition – could hardly hope to be anything but a confession of private hopes and fears. Husserl created the possibility of philosophy becoming a true science, and existentialism becoming a true philosophy.

To summarise this section of the argument:

Descartes pointed out that we never actually know objects themselves; all we know is the impact they make on our senses. It is as if consciousness were a radar screen, upon which small dots of light appear. Descartes pointed out that these dots may represent ships or aeroplanes; but we can never actually see the ships or aeroplanes themselves; only the dots on the radar screen. Husserl took what seems a very obvious step, but one that had eluded philosophers for two centuries: he asked why, in that case, do we not study the mechanics of the radar screen? If we can learn how it works, then we stand a better chance of discovering what is causing the dots. Phenomenology is the study of the radar screen.

CHAPTER THREE

THE MEANING OF HUSSERL'S REVOLUTION

The aim of Phenomenology–How Phenomenology is applied–Transactionism–Whitehead's Revolution

The real point about the phenomenological method is still to be made. Human beings are born into a world which they accept and take for granted. The world was there before they arrived, and their parents seem to know what life is all about. We all derive our ideas about ourselves from the way that other people see us, and during our early years, our personalities are little more than a passive reflection of environment (although conditioned, of course, by genetic factors). After these very early years, life becomes a series of surprises, because we are always seeing things we take for granted from other points of view. Perhaps this first shock of changing viewpoint may come from a visit to a relative, and the discovery that other people may have quite a different conception of good table manners from that of one's own parents. Every time something like this happens, another brick falls out of the claustrophobic edifice of childhood, and we receive a shock of freedom. (This may explain why most of us can never quite outgrow a certain pleasure in destruction; it remains associated with freedom.)

For a certain type of mind – the young H. G. Wells, for example – science administers the greatest of all the shocks of freedom. The whole of one's accepted world falls apart, and great streams of light come blasting in. Each of the earlier shocks of freedom was a fragmentary escape from personality, from one's conception of oneself through the eyes of other people. But this is suddenly the possibility of an almost inconceivable *total* freedom from personality. No other study can produce quite this effect: literature, music, history, all act as catalysts upon the old personality, transmuting it into something new; but the old foundations remain, for these are essentially 'human' studies, and they appeal to us *as* human beings, and emphasise that we are members of the human family. Science is knowledge of external nature, and it does not make its appeal to us as human beings. A scientist reading an article on his own subject might as well be a Martian, or a disembodied brain, or a ball of light. In the face of this completely impersonal knowledge, the fact that I happen to be a creature with two arms, two legs and a head is quite irrelevant. This, at any rate, is one's feeling when science makes its first great impact.

When we say that someone is 'only human, after all,' we are usually referring to weakness or stupidity. The scientific vision seems to hold out a possibility of human beings who are not 'human' in this sense – of 'men like gods.' Bertrand Russell expressed it in a letter written in 1918:

> 'I *must*, before I die, find *some* way to say the essential thing that is in me, that I have never said yet – a thing that is not love or hate or pity or scorn, but the very breath of life, fierce and coming from far away, bringing into human life the vastness and fearful passionless force of non-human things . . .'[1]

1. Quoted by Alan Wood. See Russell: *My Philosophical Development*, p. 261.

(It is curious that Russell should always have been so violently opposed to the philosophy of Nietzsche, which is an embodiment of this idea.)

This is essentially the vision that drives all science and philosophy.

It is inevitable that disillusionment should follow. The scientist may now be able to escape the enclosed and intensely personal world of his childhood, reject its intellectual prejudices and even destroy most of its emotional reflexes; but he remains a human being in a human body, and somehow all the knowledge in the world leaves him basically unchanged. It is a sign of Goethe's astonishing genius that he managed to express this disillusionment in *Faust* before the scientific century was really under way. For this is precisely what Faust complains about at the beginning of the drama. He has studied philosophy, medicine, law, theology, and still feels 'no wiser than before.' What is the point of knowing so much if you feel, in a basic sense, frustrated and stagnant, so that you envy the yokels dancing on the village green?

It seems, then, that the scientific vision promises something that it cannot accomplish. This is the source of the despair of the nineteenth century – expressed, for example, in Tennyson's *In Memoriam* – and ultimately of the intellectual nihilism of our own day. Science, it seemed, could not, after all, replace religion; yet its premises have administered a slow poison to religion from which it can obviously never recover. So what is to be done?

And now it is possible to see the full significance of Husserl's revolution. He points out that if philosophy finds itself in a *cul de sac*, this is simply because it has so far been a half-measure – like science. Science may appear to hurl man out of his world of provincialism and prejudice; but Husserl has shown that man's prejudices go a great deal deeper than his intellect or his emotions. Consciousness itself is 'prejudiced' – that is to say, intentional. I am born into a 'situation' that includes my family background and my social background, and I shall grow up with certain intellectual and emotional prejudices that are the result of these. Science may help me to shed most of them. But I am also born with habits of perception that have been slowly achieved over millions of years, and which science leaves untouched. Admittedly, some of these perceptions broaden as I get older: I may develop a sense for music or poetry or religion. But these things will only make clear to me what it is that torments Faust: that mere knowledge – of science, philosophy, etc. – has no radical effect upon my essential being as a glowing fragment of life, striving to be more alive. If knowledge is really to fire my *whole* being, and cause it to expand, it must not be capable merely of exploding my childhood prejudices and releasing me into a broader world of universal knowledge; it must also enable me to understand my inner-being: what happens, for example, to my consciousness when I am moved by great music. If this can be done, then the immense release that science promises can become a real possibility. In being able to stand aside from my habits of perception, I shall have discovered the secret of poetry and mysticism. Rimbaud had glimpsed this truth when he talked about 'systematic derangement of the senses'; science, after all, is the systematic derangement of human prejudice, and Husserl has showed that consciousness is also 'prejudiced'; unfortunately, Rimbaud had no idea of where to begin, and wasted time experimenting with drugs and alcohol, until his insight faded.

An animal is a passive creature; it adapts to its environment and leaves it at that. Man became an evolutionary force when he overcame the 'passive fallacy' that governs the animal's attitude: when, that is, he discovered that his efforts could change the world. A human being is a creature who has made Mr Polly's discovery: 'If you don't like your life, you can change it.' Man has reached an impasse in his evolutionary development because he has not yet made the discovery that his perception can also be changed; where consciousness is concerned, he still suffers from the 'passive fallacy' – that as things are, so they must remain.

How the Existentialists tried to use Phenomenology

Martin Heidegger, with his questioning, religious temperament, so akin to Kierkegaard's, immediately saw the possibilities of Husserl's discoveries for existentialism. Philosophy since Descartes had refused to acknowledge that man could be a fit subject for its speculations. The philosopher, said Descartes, should begin with the question: What can I know? This meant that philosophy was only concerned with man the knower – not man the lover and sufferer, the 'thinking reed' with his weakness and degradation and strange flashes of greatness. For Kierkegaard, this was a major tragedy. How, he asked, could philosophy be so stupid as to concentrate on the minor question and ignore the really great question, the *only* really important question? This was the question that hung over Kierkegaard night and day, and that produced in him at the same time both torment and ecstasy. Previous centuries had been wrong; man is not a passive creature, intended to obey the law and cultivate his garden. The literature, the music, the philosophy of the nineteenth century spoke of a new vision of man as something surging and pushing, groping towards a new state of being. Yet even Hegel, with his vision of history as a movement of the spirit, failed to grasp the whole essence of this new situation: that man was suddenly confronted with the possibility *of a new kind of freedom.* By thinking in terms of history, Hegel automatically minimised the part of the individual; but the important thing about this romantic freedom was that it *was* individual. When gripped by its power, man ceased to feel a mere unit of society, a member of a species; he became as unique as God. So there could be no philosophical system that understood this freedom, for the very notion of a system removed its essence.

But Kierkegaard felt himself driven into a corner by this incomprehension. He found the temper of the mediaeval saints more congenial; he gave way to the temptation to become a mere anti-Hegel, an anti-scientist, a neo-Christian. It was inevitable that his protest was misunderstood and ignored, for he was expressing it in a way that invited misunderstanding. After the *Unscientific Postscript* (the title itself was enough to make his contemporaries wrinkle their noses) he made no further attempt to meet the philosophers halfway; he became a preacher, a dealer in religious paradox.

Heidegger was determined not to fall into this trap; whatever happened, he would never give philosophers the chance to dismiss his ideas by declaring that they fell outside philosophy. And *Being and Time* was a magnificent opening shot in his campaign: brilliant, erudite (strung with Greek quotations), strictly phenomenological in method, and with hardly a passing reference to religion. By stating that philosophy since the Greeks has forgotten the great Question of Being (seinfrage) and that he intended to revive it. Heidegger had shifted his ground to a safe distance from religion. Few people at the time noticed that the closest relative of *Sein und Zeit*, in the emotional sense, is Pascal's *Pensées*.

Being and Time is mainly an attempt to describe the psychological (or spiritual?) problems of the poet in terms of psychology. This sentence sounds tautologous until we recognise that Heidegger meant a psychology with a strictly phenomenological method; that is, with no Freudian presumptions about the libido or the death-wish. The starting point of *Sein und Zeit* is that man finds himself tangled in psychological chains, and has only occasional glimpses of freedom – or, to use an excellent phrase of William Kimmel's, 'the fundamental alienation of beings from the source of power, meaning and purpose'.[1]

Heidegger's very anxiety to meet philosophers halfway was his undoing; he confronted the same problem as Kierkegaard: that the essence of existentialism is an *experience of freedom* so unique that the attempt to fit it into a philosophical system is self-defeating. *Sein und Zeit* was to have been in three volumes; only the first was ever published. Heidegger said that the second was written, but did not seem to him to satisfy basic standards of clarity. One can believe him. But at least, having made his reputation as a man capable of sustained thought in the western philosophical tradition, Heidegger was now able to turn to more congenial modes of expression – to attempting to express himself in strange, allusive essays on poetry, or books of impenetrable aphorisms. Heidegger very quickly abandoned the Husserlian method. The consequence is that he remains one of the most interesting and challenging of modern thinkers – yet somehow giving

1. *The Search for Being;* selected texts on existentialism, Noonday, New York, 1962.

the impression of being uncompleted, like the foundations of some enormous palace that was too expensive to finish.

The case of Sartre is similar; it was also quite apparent, from his first attempts to apply Husserl's method, that he was taking the first steps of a vicious circle.

Now Husserl had not only prescribed the method – of purely descriptive analysis of human consciousness; he had also made a statement of the ultimate aim of the phenomenologist. Science, as already remarked, has the power of freeing man from his 'false selves' – ideas about himself and the world built on childhood prejudice. Husserl suggested – naturally enough – that as man loses all the false ideas about himself and the world through scientific analysis, and as he comes to recognise that he himself is responsible for so much that he assumed to be 'objective,' he will come to recognise his true self, presiding over perception and all other acts of living. This idea seems common-sensible enough, and our intuitions about ourselves seem to support it.

Sartre, as one can gather from his autobiography, was a strangely claustrophobic personality, perpetually disgusted by itself; philosophy had upon him the effect that science had on the young Wells, of providing a sense of release, of the 'fearful passionless force of non-human things.' Husserl's phenomenology became for him, as for Heidegger, a method by which questions about man's freedom and destiny could again be brought within the pale of philosophy. But Husserl's talk about the 'transcendental ego' (i.e. the 'true self' that 'intends' all intentional acts and constitutes the world) seemed to Sartre a survival of romantic idealism, and a threat to the status of phenomenology as an academic philosophy. Sartre became *plus royaliste que le roi*, more phenomenological than Husserl, and declared that there is no such constituting ego, no 'true self.' Consciousness is not only intentional; it *is* intentionality.

This is a matter that deserves closer examination, for it is fundamental to the 'old existentialism.'

Husserl pointed out that consciousness is intentional. I do not merely see something; *I fire my attention at an object as I might fire a rifle at a target.* If I do not do this, then I am not conscious of what I am looking at.

Now Sartre goes further. He declares that to be conscious *is to be conscious of something.* 'A consciousness that ceases to be consciousness *of* something would, for that very reason, cease to exist' (*L'Imaginaire*). But is this so? I can look at a thing without seeing it, but I am still conscious. Sartre would reply: Because you are conscious of something else. Your attention is wandering elsewhere, perhaps, but it *is* somewhere. But is this so? Can I be conscious, but conscious of nothing? (to use a phrase of T. S. Eliot's). Merleau-Ponty, another eminent phenomenologist, agrees that most consciousness is intentional, but suggests that the kind of consciousness we experience on the edge of sleep is non-intentional. If I close my eyes, I may become 'conscious of nothing,' but there is a distinct difference between this consciousness of nothing, and actually falling asleep.

Sartre, however, will not have this. The usual idea of consciousness is that it is a kind of light by which we see things. But a light has to be switched on, and it has a source. According to Sartre, it has no source except the object itself; it is as if the object was luminous, so to speak. He expresses his view graphically:

'Imagine a linked series of explosions which wrench us from ourselves . . . which throw us on . . . the dry dust of the world, on the rough earth, among things; imagine that we are thus rejected, forsaken by our very nature in an indifferent, hostile and restive world; you would then know the profound meaning of the discovery that Husserl expresses in the famous phrase: "All consciousness is consciousness *of* something" '[1].

Sartre has here gone further than Husserl; he sees consciousness as something passive, a 'wind blowing towards objects,' and writes: 'if, against all impossibility, you were to enter "into" a consciousness, you would be seized by a vortex and thrown out . . . because consciousness has no "inside"; it is nothing but the outside of itself.' (*Situations*, 1, p. 31.)

Sartre felt that he was stripping Husserl's theory of all idealistic nonsense and placing existentialism on a completely scientific basis. In fact, he has simply undone everything Husserl set out to do. In the old mechanical theories of man, there was no need for consciousness, because everything that men seem to do out of 'free will' can be explained purely as response to a stimulus; consequently the psychologist Watson said that he had never observed anything that could be called consciousness! In the same way, David Hume said that when he looked inside himself for his 'true I,' he could never actually see his 'I,' but only a lot of perceptions and feelings. All that Sartre has done is to introduce an existentialist variation on this theme. Man is a Cartesian robot *with consciousness*, but his consciousness is mechanical, like the rest of him; the robot merely has a headlight set in its forehead so that it can see ahead. According to Sartre, there is no 'I' that directs consciousness; consciousness is 'I,' and it is an emptiness, a mere condition for the unity of experience.

This view was set out in Sartre's earliest philosophical

1. *Situations*, 1, p. 33. Quoted by Maurice Natanson, p. 28.

work, an essay called *The Transcendence of the Ego*. It is hard to understand how he managed to retain the view that consciousness is intentional at all, since he had reduced consciousness to something passive. Consciousness, in Sartre, is like the sea, drawn towards objects as the tide is drawn by the moon – by gravity.

There is obviously, then, a fundamental self-contradiction at the very root of Sartre's philosophy – a contradiction that is a reflection of his conflicting desires to be an existentialist and yet to remain a strict scientist. His sentence about being 'cast up' among objects and 'forsaken by our very nature' is a picture of what he calls 'nausea' in the novel of that title, and we have already gone into the question of why Sartre's response to 'naked existence' is so unlike that of Heidegger or Aldous Huxley. Here again, then, in his phenomenology as well as in his existentialism, Sartre's temperament – his tendency to be anti-emotional because he is frightened of emotion – betrays him into an attitude that weakens the foundations of his philosophy.

The aim of Phenomenology

The above remarks on Heidegger and Sartre were by way of a digression, an attempt to explain how they attempted to apply phenomenological techniques, and in what manner they failed. Heidegger has certainly remained truer to the Husserlian spirit in phenomenology – the spirit that should be the basis of a thoroughgoing existentialism. For both Husserl and Heidegger were driven by a certain optimistic intuition: that somehow, man would discover the secret of the working of consciousness, and become for the first time a truly free creature, a truly *human* creature, if we define an animal as a creature of stimulus and response. In *Nausea*, Sartre says of a moronic café proprietor, 'When his café empties, his head empties, too.' That is to say, his consciousness *is* completely dependent on external objects to draw it forth; when these vanish, it goes to sleep. This should have led Sartre to recognise that a more satisfactory kind of man would be less dependent on objects, more capable of controlling his consciousness. But the idea of 'controlling consciousness' suggests a 'controller,' and this Sartre could not allow.

Both Husserl and Heidegger felt that the phenomenological quest would give man the possibility of 'mystical' experience without the need for specifically Christian or Yogic disciplines. Husserl said that the study of intentionality in action would lead towards the 'keepers of the key to the ultimate sources of being' (a thoroughly Heideggerian phrase), and to the 'unveiling of the hidden achievements of the transcendental ego.'

How Phenomenology is applied

Now it is necessary to say something more about the disciplines of phenomenology, and their actual aims. It should be admitted at once that there are as many different kinds of phenomenology as there are phenomenologists. This is as it should be. Phenomenology is a method; in fact, it is little more than another name for science, an attempt at the most rigorous form of science. Different scientists have different aims, different fields to which they apply the scientific method; so it is with phenomenology. One of the most important of modern phenomenologists, Roman Ingarden, spent his life applying phenomenology to the art-work; Merleau-Ponty was concerned with the phenomenological analysis of the body as a giver-of-meaning. Psychotherapy is a particularly rich field for the application of phenomenology – in fact, perhaps the richest of all. Whatever its field, phenomenology is an attempt to observe things as an emanation of consciousness, and ultimately to increase the control of the human being over his own existence.

It will be seen at once that Husserl's aim is basically identical with that of Jaspers. Jaspers wants us to grasp knowledge as a living process, and the human relation to it as dynamic – so that we throw off the old fallacy that we are passive creatures in the face of it. A child might be overawed by a great city, but a civil engineer knows that he might demolish it and rebuild it himself. Husserl's philosophy has the same aim: to show us that, although we may have been thrust into this world without a 'by your leave,' we are mistaken to assume that it exists independently of us. It is true that reality exists apart from us; but what we mistake for *the* world is actually *a* world constituted by us, selected from an infinitely complex reality. It is there, just as a city is there. But the city was built by our fathers, and our world was built, was *chosen*, by our ancestors, who passed on their vision to us in the genes. A city is a convenient place to live in, which is why it was built. But if we are living in a city that depresses us with its ugliness, we can move to another one (or even build our own). The same is true of the constituted life-world into which we are born (and which Sartre, for example, shows a persistent tendency to identify as *the* world).

What does a phenomenologist actually *do*? He applies the phenomenological method to whatever may be his own field. Something must be said briefly about this phenomenological method.

If I am listening to a piece of music which excites me, I am aware of it purely as *meaning*, i.e. what it is doing to me. If I happen also to be a musical scholar, I may well recognise, at the same time, precisely how the composer is managing to move or excite me. But if I get too curious about this latter aspect, and turn my attention upon the mechanics of the music, I shall cease to feel its meaning, and cease to enjoy it so deeply.

Now this world in which I live is very much like a piece of music. My day proceeds like a symphony, with dull passages and exciting passages, passages that arouse sadness, passages that arouse rage or determination, passages that almost lose my attention entirely. My 'life world' – the world of my lived experience – presents itself to me as a series of meanings or half-meanings. But just as I can turn my attention from the meaning of a symphony to its mechanics, so I can examine the structure of my experience, of my 'life world.' The phenomenologist is the counterpart of the musical theorist who is interested to find out how the composer achieved his effects. But with this important difference: the phenomenologist is aware that *he himself is the composer*.

Music, then, has two levels, and we can switch from one to the other. If I wish to concentrate entirely on the mechanics of the music I shall have to try to prevent being moved by it at all, because this will distract me. Husserl calls this process of concentrating on the structure of the music 'bracketing.' I 'bracket out' the meaning, and concentrate on its structure. Husserl calls each act of bracketing an '*epoché*.' (I mention these technical terms, not because I propose to make use of them myself, but in case the reader is using this account as a general introduction to phenomenology.) The first *epoché* consists of bracketing out one's belief in the real existence of the object under examination (or the feeling, or whatever it is). I do not say 'That is a book'; I suspend my belief in its real existence, and say; 'I see a red parallelogram that appears to be an inch deep.' (Where describing emotions are concerned, it can be seen that this method would make for honesty.) The book may be a mirage or hallucination or projected on a screen by a movie-camera; I do not ask about this. That is the first *epoché*.

There are still various levels of the object that can be 'bracketed out.' For example, if I am looking at a Victorian painting that tells a story, I may first bracket out my awareness of it as a story, then as a picture containing human figures, so that I see it now simply as a design, a structure; I may even bracket out my awareness of its colours, until I see it as a pure structure. These are three levels that can be suspended in successive *epochés*.

Transactionism

In recent years, a group of American psychologists who call themselves 'transactionists' have been pursuing a line of investigation that is essentially practical phenomenology, and it may bring the discussion down to earth at this point if I speak about their work.[1]

Transactionism is a psychology of perception, based upon the recognition that there is no such thing as 'simple perception' – i.e. perception that is not intentional. Perception is not a passive activity, which only requires the opening of the eyes; it is a transaction with the environment, like going into a shop and buying a pound of butter. This statement will not cause any difficulty for anyone who has understood the preceding chapter.

What is original about transactionism is some of the experiments devised to show that perception is a transaction. We are all familiar with certain errors of perception; for example, if I am sitting in a train in a station, and the

1. The most prominent names in this movement are those of the late Adelbert Ames, Jnr., Hadley Cantril, William H. Ittelson and Franklin P. Kilpatrick.

train alongside me starts up, I assume for a moment that it is my own train that is moving, and have to turn my head to look at the platform before I can convince my eyes that I am still stationary.

In fact, 'perception' is at least fifty per cent *assumptions*, and these assumptions depend on the total circumstances in which the perception takes place. For example, if I am sitting in the station master's office looking out of the window and I see a train start up, I do not have a moment of doubt about whether I am moving because I am not *expecting* to move.

In a book called *Symbolism, Its Meaning and Effect*, Whitehead pointed out that perception is usually a matter of symbols, just like language; I say I see a book when I actually see a red oblong. The Transactionists (who have been influenced by Whitehead rather than Husserl) take this one stage further, and point out that when I 'perceive' something, I am usually making a *bet* with myself that what I perceive is what I think it is. In order to act and live at all, I have to make these bets; I cannot afford to make absolutely certain that things are what I think they are. But this means that we should not take our perceptions at their face value, any more than Nietzsche was willing to accept philosophy at its face value; we must allow for prejudice and distortion.

One of the most effective experiments devised by the transactionists was the 'distorted room.' If I take a photograph of a man who is lying down, with the camera close to his feet, the photograph will show a man with enormous feet and a tiny head. Now supposing someone shows me such a photograph of a man with enormous feet and a small head. I say to him: 'You have held the camera too close to his feet,' but the photographer replies: 'No, as a matter of fact, he is a man with outsize feet. . . .'

In the distorted room experiment, this principle is applied. I am led to a small peephole in a screen. I look through it, and see what appears to be an ordinary room. Standing in one corner is a small boy, and in the other, a tall man. There are also a couple of chairs standing somewhere near the rear wall. Now the man and the small boy advance towards one another. As they do so, they *appear to change size*, and when they reach opposite corners, their roles are reversed. The boy is now enormous, and the man has shrunk to half his size.

It is a trick of perspective. I assumed it to be a normal, square room because the wall facing me appeared to be an ordinary square. In fact, the wall was really trapeze-shaped as shown below:

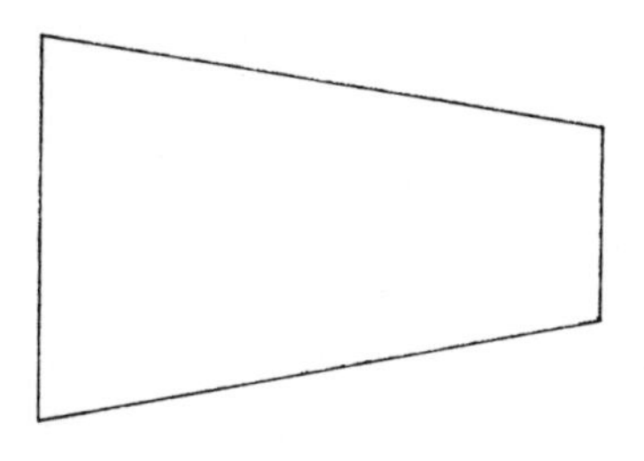

But what I did not realise was that it was *sloping away from me*, so that the short end of the trapezium was closest to my eye, so that it appeared to be exactly the same length as the long end. (The principle is the same as in photographing the man with big feet.) Consequently I appeared to be looking at an ordinary rectangle. Sometimes, there are two windows in the wall, also trapeze-shaped, so that they also appear to be square. This can lead to startling effects; if a man's face looks at me first through one window, then, a moment later, through the other, it seems to me that his head has suddenly changed size. The chairs in the room, of course, are constructed on this same 'distorted' principle.

Adelbert Ames constructed another interesting apparatus made up of a large trapezoid with numerous windows painted on it. Shadows are also painted on to enhance the illusion that the trapezoid is a square. When this apparatus is suspended on a string, and made to revolve, it actually appears to be oscillating back and forth through an angle of about 100°. If a tube is pushed through one of the windows at an angle, the tube is seen to go on moving normally while the window appears to be turning back. It follows that at certain points, the tube appears to bend.

These experiments may be dismissed – as they are by certain English psychologists – as mere experiments in illusion. But they help to make us practically aware of the truth of some of the assertions of phenomenology – particularly the central one, that our perceptions are as liable to prejudice and distortion as our emotions. One curious result to emerge from these experiments is known as the 'Honi phenomenon.' It has already been remarked that if there are two windows in the wall of the distorted room, a man's face appearing first at one then at the other will appear to change size. But in one case, a woman saw no such change in the face of the man at the two windows. The reason was that she was married to him; not only that, but they had been married for a long time, and the husband was a most distinguished man whom the wife respected. Her emotional attitude to her husband was such that she observed no change, either when his face moved from window to window, or when he walked from corner to corner of the distorted room. One presumes that the wife was able to perceive that the room *was* distorted when her husband failed to change size.

Similar experiments were tried with navy personnel; this time, the man in the distorted room was sometimes a recruit, sometimes an 'authority figure' – an N.C.O. or officer. If the observer was a recruit, it was discovered that the 'Honi effect' again occurred: that is, an authority figure was less distorted than a recruit. ('Honi' was the wife's nickname for the husband in the original experiment.) Here it can be seen that perception is altered by the mental attitude of the perceiver to the perceived. These experiments amount to a harmless and temporary form of 'brain washing'. Their results are summarised by Hadley Cantril:

'Perceiving, then, can never be an absolute disclosure of reality; instead, it reveals only a possibility, a "best bet" as to what and where the external objects are, and what their characteristics are.' (*Reflections on the Human Venture*, p. 45.)

It is the 'Honi phenomenon' that points to the possible importance of Cantril's line of approach. We assume the world to be 'what it is,' something permanent and real and stable, of far more importance than our insignificant and impermanent selves. If we want to change our perceptions, we have to get drunk or take drugs. We know that Van Gogh saw cypress trees as living torches, a starry night as a vortex of life and creative energy; but we are inclined to believe, like Camus, that such perception is 'abnormal,' and certainly of no relevance to the way we live. The Honi phenomenon indicates that the perception of quite ordinary people is affected by their unconscious assumptions. In the case of the naval recruits, the attitude that influenced their perception was the negative one of fear, but in the case of the wife, the positive one of love and respect. Is it not possible that it is Van Gogh's vision that should be called 'normal' (i.e. truer to the underlying reality of the perceived) while our everyday perception, which we assume to reveal 'reality' to us – an extremely dull reality for the most part – is distorted by thoroughly negative assumptions such as fear, boredom, assumption of our own insignificance? Fifty years ago, such a question would have been regarded as hopelessly idealistic and unscientific; nowadays, because of the work of men like Cantril, Maslow and the existential psychologists (of whom I shall speak later), it has a meaning that can be tested in the laboratory.

The phrase 'truer to the underlying reality of the perceived' may strike some readers as an attempt at verbal sleight of hand; after all, why call either vision 'normal,' when we admit that vision depends upon what we put into it? But to think in this manner is to fail to grasp the full implication of the phenomenological outlook. It is true that our perception is thoroughly prejudiced and selective. But then, in a sense, the 'reality' out there is a buzzing chaos, like the sounds of an orchestra tuning up. Through millions of years of evolution, we have developed a capacity for distinguishing the different instruments; our senses 'filter off' a great deal of the chaos so that it never reaches us; our nervous systems handle the rest to give it meaning. But our perception is still a second best, many degrees better than the original chaos, but a long way from its *possibilities* of seeing order and meaning in the universe. We might express the state of affairs by saying that the present 'order' that reigns in our perceptions is a kind of martial law. Life is not easy; it is too complicated, so we have to limit our perceptions to cope with it, just as an army commander has to declare martial law in a city that might get completely out of hand at any moment; but no one pretends that martial law is an ideal condition for nurturing a City of the Sun. The martial law has led to what Heidegger calls 'forgetfulness of existence.' So it is no loose thinking to use a phrase like 'truer to the underlying reality' in the phenomenological sense. The error arises from the old assumption that perception is passive, and that therefore it is a purely relative matter which we regard as 'normal.' All perception is intentional; Van Gogh's perception is *more* intentional than our everyday perception, and since there could be no perception without intentionality, it is not at all a relative matter, but a matter of life and death. No intentionality, no perception.

To readers who have followed this argument closely, it will be recognised that ideas of momentous import are being suggested. The change to the 'phenomenological viewpoint' may be a difficult one to grasp, just as the difference between Einsteinian physics and Newtonian physics seemed irritatingly elusive at the beginning of this century; but the consequences of the change of viewpoint are as momentous in both cases. Phenomenology is a Copernican revolution in thought, whose full implications were hidden even from its founder Husserl. Expressed fifty years ago, some of its central concepts would have sounded 'anti-scientific' in the sense that Blake or D. H. Lawrence were anti-scientific. But all that has really happened is that science has revised its foundations with the idea of removing anomalies and contradictions, and has made itself more 'scientific' than ever. It was the old concept of science as merely objective observation that was unscientific.

Whitehead's Revolution

Whitehead, who knew little or nothing of Husserl's work, nevertheless reached conclusions that are fundamentally similar, and it is perhaps worth another brief digression to mention these. In *Symbolism, Its Meaning and Effect*, he suggested that we are mistaken to think that we possess only one mode of perception – our 'immediacy perception' of things. I certainly possess this mode of perception – which could be described as a kind of feeler reaching out from my eyes, and feeling its way over the surface of the things around me. But I possess a *second* mode of perception, which can hardly be described by a simile, except perhaps to say that it is like switching on an electric light in a dark room and suddenly revealing a whole situation that it would have taken hours to assess by 'feeling' around the room in the dark. In other words, we possess *meaning perception*, and the two modes of perception have to work together. Another analogy will help to make the meaning of this clearer. During the war, when it was a question of destroying certain dams in Germany, the R.A.F. was confronted with the problem of how an aircraft could be made to fly very low over a lake at a precisely determined height. It was obviously no solution to suggest trailing a long ruler from the underside of the aeroplane down to the surface of the water. Then someone suggested the obvious and simple solution: to install two spotlights, one in the nose and one in the tail of the plane, whose beams would converge at precisely the right distance under the plane. All the pilot then had to do was to switch on both lights, and when both beams made a single circle on the water, keep the plane at exactly that height.

We are inclined to think of perception as a single beam that emanates from the eye and goes out to objects. But that is only one mode of perception – immediacy. To really perceive something, both 'modes' have to be switched on simultaneously, and when they converge perfectly upon the object, then we truly 'perceive' it.

Sometimes, if we are very tired or nervously prostrated, meaning-perception vanishes almost completely, and then we merely 'see' things, but they are without meaning. The hero of Sartre's *Nausea* was in this position. Mostly, both my modes of perception work, but they fail to converge precisely on the object. This is because 'meaning perception' works best at a distance, and immediacy perception works best at close quarters, and I am seldom at exactly the right distance for them to be equal. Apart from which, every fluctuation in my mental energy means that meaning perception gets dimmer and immediacy perception increases. In certain moments of intense excitement or pleasure, it may happen the other way around, and then I experience the opposite of 'forgetfulness of existence,' a sense that all the meanings of my world are intensified. Or, to use another simile, my everyday experience is like playing a piano with my foot firmly on the pedal that muffles the notes, so that every note dies out as soon as it has struck, and there is no sense of continuity. When my meaning perception intensifies, it is as if I had taken my foot off the pedal; each note goes on vibrating, so that we now get an orchestral effect, in which meanings seem to spread outwards like ripples on a pond.

The usual scientific viewpoint would have it that we have only one mode of perception – immediacy – and meanings are not something we perceive, but something we *infer* with our minds by adding together individual sensations we have perceived, in the way that a mathematician gets a result by adding up every figure in a column. But this is not quite true. It is true that most accountants concern themselves with one figure at a time, and the adding up is purely a mental process; but it is easy to imagine a mathematician who is so brilliant that a column of figures presents itself to him pictorially, and he *sees* the answer in a flash. He may then confirm it by the more laborious method, but the adding-up process is only a lengthy way of arriving at the meaning he has seen in a flash.

The above is a necessarily brief, and perhaps somewhat distorted, version of Whitehead's thesis in *Symbolism*. Whitehead's argument begins as an attack on Hume and his criticism of cause and effect (mentioned earlier), so that he calls meaning-perception 'causal efficacy,' and immediacy perception 'presentational immediacy.' All that is important to grasp at the moment is the concept of perception as a *focussing* of two 'beams' of perception. (Again, the interpretation of the concept in these terms is my own.) The full significance of this will emerge in the second part of this book.

The 'two modes of perception,' incidentally, need not be accepted as a literal account of the way perception works, but simply as a model that helps us to grasp its workings. To some extent it obviously conflicts with phenomenology, for 'meaning perception' is another name for intentionality, and the phenomenologist holds that there is no perception without intentionality.

What, finally, then, is the point of all this discussion about the mechanism of perception? How is it related to the problems of human freedom and the fundamental 'life question'[1] that tormented Pascal and Kierkegaard? I shall try to make this clear in the following chapter.

1. I prefer the term 'life question' or 'lebensfrage' to Heidegger's 'seinfrage,' which is of narrower application.

CHAPTER FOUR

THE NEW PICTURE OF THE UNIVERSE

The need to know–Existential psychology–
The case of 'Maria'–Peak experiences in psychotherapy–
Alcoholics cured by mescalin and LSD

The present chapter will conclude the work of 'preparing the ground' for a consideration of the problems of a 'new existentialism.'

I have tried to show so far that a quiet but fundamental revolution has occurred in our idea of science. The scientist of the nineteenth century saw himself, to some extent, as a man fighting a battle against the forces of self-delusion and obscurity. His picture of himself tended to be an extreme reaction; ranged against him he saw the church, with its torturers and inquisitors, and the State, whose interest lay in keeping the people ignorant and oppressed. As a consequence, it became an article of the scientific faith that man habitually overrates his own importance in a universe that is unaware of his existence. Religions distort the truth about man to conform to wishful thinking; the scientist declared: 'My truth lies out there, in nature or in space; my method of arriving at it – disinterested observation and the use of my reason.' He pictured the ideal scientist as a kind of combination of camera and adding machine. Religion overrated man; science automatically did the opposite. Religion declared man had an immortal soul; science said he was a machine.

Religion said man was the special object of God's attention; science said he was a chance product of a non-purposive evolution. Religion said that man could sin or be virtuous of his own free will; science said that man was a penny-in-the-slot machine with no free will. Strindberg voiced the objection to all this when he quoted St Martin:

'[Men] have believed themselves to be obeying the dictates of humility when they have denied that the earth and all that the universe contains exists only on man's account, on the grounds that the admission of such an idea would be only conceit. *But they have not been afraid of the laziness and cowardice that are the inevitable results of this false modesty.*' (*Legends* (1912), p. 74.)

The modern scientist is simply coming to recognise that this vision of science was as lop-sided and prejudiced, in its way, as the vision it set out to displace. If the ideal scientist was a machine, a camera with an adding machine attached, *what drove it to seek truth*? Something had obviously been left out, something very personal. This has recently been pointed out brilliantly by Michael Polanyi, an eminent physicist, in his book *Personal Knowledge* whose thesis is that the 'strict objectivity' of science is a delusion. 'Even in the exact sciences, "knowing" is an art, of which the skill of the knower, guided by his passionate sense of increasing contact with reality, is a logically necessary part.'

What is in question is the *driving force* behind science. The nineteenth-century scientist may, to the best of his knowledge, have been telling the truth when he talked about a purely objective desire for knowledge; but if so, it was only because he has, at the back of his mind, a picture of the power of the forces of anti-knowledge. Even in a book like Bertrand Russell's *Religion and Science* there is a tendency to glorify science by dwelling on the wicked old days when a scientist could be burnt at the stake, rather as Russian communists dwell on the evil days of Tsarism. In these days, when science has won its battle, it has lost the power of this negative drive, and the scientist can see that the 'objective desire for knowledge' was never an adequate explanation of the tremendous vitality of science. Knowledge *for* what? Not for its own sake, but for some passionate and personal urge to establish contact with reality and to convert the knower into something greater than an adding machine.

The need to know

This brings the discussion back to Professor Maslow. In an interesting paper called *The Need to Know and the Fear of Knowing*, Maslow relates how, in 1932, he was working on delayed reactions in monkeys, and asked himself why the monkeys worked at certain boring problems. It was not the piece of bread they got as a reward, for they would sometimes solve the problem and then throw the food away. They worked almost as well for little blocks of wood, or for no reward at all.

Six years later, one of Maslow's patients was a college girl who complained of various nervous ailments, all of which amounted to a total loss of interest in life – what William James has called 'anhedonia'; the boredom even expressed itself physically in failure to menstruate. She explained that she had left college and hoped to continue at some line of work that would demand her full intelligence. It was the time of the depression, and by a stroke of luck she found an excellent job at a good wage in a chewing-gum factory, which enabled her to take care of her unemployed family.

Instead of analysing the girl's childhood frustrations and traumas in the classic Freudian manner, Maslow made the sensible suggestion that such an intelligent girl might be feeling a fundamental frustration at her failure to use her mind; he suggested part-time studies. The remedy worked; the girl regained her zest for life, and the physical symptoms disappeared.

This, and similar cases, led Maslow to a conclusion that is close to Michael Polanyi's: that the need to know is a burning drive that is not necessarily a manifestation of more important drives – the need for security, etc. *It is a primary psychological drive in its own right.* 'Direct examination of psychologically healthy people shows pretty clearly that they are positively attracted to the mysterious, to the unknown, to the puzzling and the unexplained. This . . . contrasts sharply with the psychologically sick person's tendency to be threatened by the unfamiliar, the ambiguous . . .' (Nietzsche's first book suggests that Greek tragedy was a manifestation of their overwhelming zest for living.) Maslow points out that gratification of this need to know is satisfying even when it yields painful results. The healthy person wants truth even if it is painful; only the unhealthy indulge in 'bad faith' for self-protection.

The revolutionary implications of this may not be apparent at first sight. It means that the fundamental drive of human life is not some Freudian libido or death-wish, nor the fear of the unknown and the need for security, but an *evolutionary appetite* of which the other appetites are minimum-manifestations. (That is to say that fear or the need for security becomes a fundamental drive only when the vital forces are in retreat and a defensive battle is the best that can be managed.) Maslow does not use the phrase 'evolutionary appetite,' but this is clearly implied.

To readers of a hundred years from now, all this may seem too obvious to need saying. But psychology in the mid-twentieth century is still based on assumptions derived from Freud and from nineteenth-century mechanism. Men are driven by the 'three S's – self, sex and society, and most psychological illness is caused by the maladjustment of the self to sex or society. Once this adjustment is achieved, the only urge of importance that is left is the will to dominate, to establish superiority over the rest of society. It is a negative picture. George Orwell pointed out in an essay on *No Orchids for Miss Blandish* that this highly unpleasant gangster thriller is only a translation into fictional terms of the 'realist' ethic and philosophy of our day. (The same might be said of the James Bond thrillers of the late fifties.) The moral atmosphere of these books, with their violence and sadism, is the moral atmosphere of nineteenth-century science with its element of 'reactionary idealism' (against religious and political oppression) subtracted. Just as behind Chaucer there seems to stretch the whole panorama of the mediaeval church; just as behind Dickens there is the whole weight of British protestantism and humanism; so behind Hadley Chase or Ian Fleming there stretches the universe of nineteenth-century science, in which the earth is a grain of sand in an empty universe, and man is an evolutionary accident who was clever enough to feed on the animal who wanted to feed on him.

It might be objected that all psychology recognises the importance of the 'need to know'; after all, it was Freud who demonstrated that neuroses could be cured by giving the patient an insight into their causes. But in this picture, the need to know is still a mere servant of the will to survival. The implications of Maslow's views goes much further. In 1914, Shaw used the phrase '... an appetite for fruitful activity and a high quality of life.' If the 'need to know' is simply one manifestation of this appetite (although perhaps the most important), then it will be seen why it cannot be interpreted as a part of the will to survival and self-assertion. The chief characteristic of the human being is that his interests extend far beyond mere survival and comfort. The need for survival is a mere sub-department of the 'appetite for fruitful activity and a high quality of life.'

Here it must be admitted that I am using the word 'human' in a special sense. Sartre's café proprietor whose head empties when his café empties is human in the biological sense. But recent centuries are seeing the whole-sale emergence of a type of human being whose 'minimum requirements' go beyond a full stomach and a compliant sexual partner. In his autobiography, H. G. Wells comments that people can now ask a question that would have been incomprehensible five hundred years ago. 'They can say: "Yes, you earn a living, you support a family, you love and hate, but – *what do you do*?" ' This life of the mind becomes increasingly important to increasing numbers of people, and Wells goes on: 'I do not now in the least desire to live longer unless I can go on with what I consider to be my proper business.' That is to say that Wells's minimum requirement from life is not mere survival, or even sexual or social self-assertion, but his 'originative intellectual work' that has become the whole meaning of his life. He said: 'We are like early amphibians, so to speak, struggling out of the waters that have hitherto covered our kind, into the air, seeking to breathe in a new fashion.'

To historians of the future, it may well appear that the year 1800 is roughly the dividing line between the old and the new epoch. Large numbers of these creatures with a new 'minimum requirement' begin to appear in the western world, and profoundly affect the whole life of the epoch. Judged by purely animal standards – there is something paradoxical about these 'romantics,' and they themselves recognise this, and wonder whether their strange appetite for mental freedom is not a disguised suicidal urge. (It was for this reason that I coined the word 'outsiders' to describe them.)

The reasons for this change do not concern us here. It may be, as Wells suggests, simply that the increased leisure in modern society leads people to seek new satisfactions. Or it may be that since orthodox religion is disappearing, the religious urge is re-appearing in a new form. Whatever the reason, the emergence of the 'amphibian' is a historical fact. Sartre's café proprietor is still a sea creature, whose mental life is a reflection of his environment; he is incapable of supporting the burden of his mind without help from outside. The 'amphibian' aims at a new degree of freedom, but he is by no means yet a land creature; the burden of his mind quickly exhausts him, and he is glad to return to the sea – to everyday preoccupations that support some of the weight of freedom. But it is clear that the word 'human' no longer covers the café proprietor and the land creature that the amphibian might one day become. The truly human will indicate an entirely new degree of freedom. The problem that is of importance at the moment is how this can be *made* to happen.

Existential Psychology

Professor Maslow would describe himself as an existential psychologist, and this is reflected in the title of one of his most important books, *Towards a Psychology of Being*. The word being is used here in the sense in which Heidegger uses it.

Over the past twenty-five years, a world-wide school

of existential psychologists has sprung up. Their common assumption is that psychological illnesses cannot be explained entirely in terms of social or sexual maladjustment. Some of these psychologists – Erwin Straus, Eugene Minkowski and V. E. von Gebsattel – are influenced chiefly by Husserl; others – notably Ludwig Binswanger and Medard Boss – derive more closely from Heidegger. One of the leading members of this movement, Viktor E. Frankl, was confined in a Nazi concentration camp throughout the war, and simply observed that the prisoners with the best chance of survival were not those with the strongest animal will to survival or self-assertion, but those who were supported by some sense of purpose or belief. It need not be a religious purpose; it may be an interest in mathematics, that led Jacob Trachtenberg to create his system of swift calculation in a concentration camp; or simply in human motivation, like Frankl's. Subsequently, Frankl made the same discovery in therapy that Maslow made separately: that certain neuroses responded to treatment only when problems centring about *the meaning of human existence* were faced.

Existential psychology, in fact, is simply a psychology that recognises that Maslow's 'need to know,' Shaw's 'appetite for a high quality of existence,' are as fundamental to human beings as the sexual appetite or the need for social security. (Here, of course, the word 'human' is used in the sense defined above.) In Heidegger's language, a human being is characterised by a need for contact with 'existence'; with the reality that underlies the banality of our social existence.

One immediately notices a certain difference in quality in studying case reports of existential psychologists when compared with the kind to which we have become accustomed in the works of Freud. Freud shows a distinct tendency to 'reductionism,' to cut men of genius down to size (as in his analyses of Leonardo or Dostoevsky) and to deny the reality of idealistic or creative impulses.[1] The existential psychologist is inclined simply to accept that creative frustration may be as important a cause of neurosis as the usual negative fears and anxieties. And what is important here is to understand what is meant by 'creative.' True creation is always related to self-development – in fact, is almost synonymous with it. Self-development is always related to the meaning of one's existence. The phrase 'meaning of existence' may have a very broad and obvious meaning, as in the work of Kierkegaard or Heidegger, or a very narrow one – as, for example, in the life of some totally untalented individual whose mental health is nevertheless bound up with his love of freshwater fishing. But even in this latter case, it is possible to see that the fishing is bound up with genuine creative elements – solitude, individual enterprise, communion with nature – that, in fact, are connected with the sense of the meaning of existence, even if the impulse is so feeble that the question never really has a chance to emerge. It can also be seen that a Freudian psychologist who saw the fishing as an outlet for aggression, or a symbolic sexual act, would be ignoring the most important element in the case.

The Case of 'Maria'

A case cited by Medard Boss[2] brings out the point I am trying to make here, even though its cure was affected by

1. Although the late Ernest Jones pointed out to me that Freud continually changed his standpoint – he was the reverse of a dogmatist – and his later works reveal the emergence of an increasingly non-determinist standpoint.

2. *Psychoanalysis and Daseinsanalysis*, Basic Books, New York, p. 155.

normal psychoanalytic treatment. The patient, Maria, was brought up in an atmosphere of narrow prudishness in a small Swiss village. Her mother was enormously fat, and when Maria began to develop signs of obesity in her early teens, the first neurotic symptoms appeared – the mere smell of food began to make her feel sick. She became physically emaciated and ceased to menstruate. At seventeen she went to a teachers' training college and started a rather ethereal friendship with a male student who was as thin as herself; they read great quantities of poetry to one another, and soon she regained weight and began to menstruate again. Unfortunately, she went to a dance on her nineteenth birthday, and someone tried to rape her. Following this incident – which profoundly shocked her – she suddenly developed an insurmountable aversion for her former boy-friend. A few weeks later she had a curious attack of hysteria, when she fell on the floor, twisted backwards, and began making rhythmic movements with her pelvis; when she recovered she smiled at the doctor with a 'sweetish, erotic smile.' But attempts to treat her for hysteria led to new symptoms – a strong vaginal discharge. This was cured by yet another doctor by means of hypnosis, and the symptoms changed to heart convulsions. Then she began to eat enormously – obviously suspecting that the whole thing began with her fear of growing as fat as her mother – and the heart symptoms disappeared when she became very fat. But this was also obviously the wrong solution, for her vitality now lessened to such an extent that she was advised to diet. She found this impossible – eating had become an obsession. She had formerly been noted for her great vitality and her love of her teaching work; now neurotic disturbances so overwhelmed her that psychoanalysis was advised.

Boss does not describe the method of psychoanalytic treatment, which went on for four years. But apparently this succeeded. An impressive dream announced her imminent recovery. She is at her psychiatrist's, when a man with an intelligent face enters. They leave together, and go to a festive party. There they go out on to a balcony to admire the night. 'They know that they are united in their thoughts and hearts. There is no sexual urge. They know they will marry. . . . Now the sky begins to take up the festive theme. The stars arrange themselves to form a huge Christmas tree. A powerful organ of the spheres plays a melody of peace on earth. The dreamer falls into a deep sleep from which she awakens in a mood of happiness.' Boss adds that the dream later became a reality when the patient married a very gifted professor whom she had not known at the time of dreaming, and from then on experienced no difficulty in living a life that was satisfactory in the emotional and physical sense. Her weight again became normal.

If there was no other evidence, the dream itself would indicate that Maria was a person with strong creative and idealistic impulses. She also possessed a strong capacity to love – and in her childhood, this was directed mostly at her mother, whom she constantly followed around. Fear of obesity turned this love into disgust, and sharply checked an important source of emotional satisfaction. Even so, and in spite of her neurosis about food, her creative energy found outlet in her training as a teacher, and she was noted for the enormous enthusiasm with which she approached the work. It is highly significant that she had a period of normal development, free of neurosis, when she became friendly with the lover of poetry; her creativity was now allowed full expression.

Unfortunately, the friendship had no physical component; it remained strictly platonic. The healthy physical appetites had to be suppressed – and here her family and social background must have played their part in leading her to repress them. The attempted rape produced an ambiguous reaction of disgust and desire, and the hysterical symptoms followed: the writhing on the floor, the vaginal discharges and the heart palpitations.

Up to this point, the girl's creative energy had been fighting back against the disorders; now, in exhaustion, and perhaps afraid of total insanity, she tries the effect of total capitulation – of overeating. But it is dangerous to betray the creative energies: the result is life-fatigue, anhedonia. And the dream that finally signalises the girl's recovery indicates that the energies of optimism and creation are once again working normally; the description of the stars arranging themselves into the shape of a Christmas tree has the true creative pulse about it; it expresses the same energy as a Beethoven symphony or Van Gogh's *Starry Night*.

The neurosis here was clearly due to the sexual frustration. The patient's emotional life has three powerful components: Love (of her mother), sexual desire and creative energy. When the first is frustrated, she is able to maintain her balance through creative activity. (Boss interprets the heart palpitations as a sign of the frustrated energies of affections – the heart being 'full enough to burst.') But the frustration of the sexual energies is too much. Boss does not describe his treatment of the patient, but since he refers to it as psychoanalytic, one may perhaps assume that it concentrated on the sexual aspect of the neurosis. Once the patient could be reconciled to this, the creative energies could again be freed.

I have devoted a great deal of space to this case because

it indicates, even more clearly than in the case of Maslow's girl student, the importance of the creative energies. It emphasises that we can make no greater mistake than to think of mental sickness as if it could be compared to simple physical illness. Ninety-five per cent of people suffering from a sore throat can be cured with penicillin tablets because the penicillin destroys the germ that causes a sore throat. It is almost as simple a matter as curing a squeaking door by oiling the hinge. In the case of Maria, the girl's ability to utilise her energies in creative work meant that her free will counted for more than in simple physical illnesses. She could *choose* whether to make even greater efforts to sublimate her sexual energies in poetry or teaching, and choose when to stop willing and attempt to cure herself by giving way completely to neurosis.

Existential psychology recognises how great is this element in most human beings. Man finds himself in a condition that is not completely predetermined. 'To live fully' is not simply a matter of satisfying certain desires which are natural to him as a human being; it demands an exercise of *freedom.*

Peak experiences in psychotherapy

In a paper called *Fusions of Facts and Values*, Professor Maslow mentions an experiment that could have some far-reaching repercussions. In three universities, alcoholics have been treated with mescalin or lysergic acid – *and cures were effected in sixty per cent of the cases.* He goes on to remark that almost all the patients who recovered had had a 'peak experience,' and the forty per cent who did not recover did not have a peak experience under mescalin. Apparently the peak experiences were not simply the result of the drug; they were induced by means of music, visual stimuli, words or suggestions, while the patients were under the influence of the drug.

The all-important question is obviously: Why? A little reflection will reveal the reason. The alcoholic is the man for whom everyday life has become either too boring or too painful to be worth the effort. And since his mental energy has sunk to a low level, he sees the world as essentially dead, passive. He has long since ceased to make the creative effort that kept Boss's patient Maria sane in spite of her frustrations.

A certain percentage of alcoholics are men who are too brutalised or stupid to enjoy any pleasure that is not largely physical. But a very large percentage are certainly over-sensitive individuals who shrink from the impact of reality. Charles Jackson portrays an alcoholic of this type in *The Lost Weekend*, a man who dramatises himself as a kind of modern Edgar Allan Poe. For most of us, life has lengthy dull passages, but sheer activity often stops us from noticing them too much. For a man whose mental energies have sunk to a point where he is no longer able to contribute the necessary concentration even to reading a book or watching television, drink provides a momentary sensation of 'fruitful activity and a high quality of life.' Unfortunately, heavy drinking is also a depressive, so the stimulating effects are lost in the hangover, the only cure for which is more drink.

The effects of mescalin or LSD can be, in some respects, far more satisfying than those of alcohol. To begin with, they last longer; they also leave behind no hangover, and leave the mental faculties clear and unimpaired. They stimulate the faculties and produce the ideal ground for a peak experience.

Now the peak experience might be described as a kind of orgasm of creative, as distinguished from sexual, energy. Creation is man's clearest awareness of his freedom. The peak experience – aided by LSD – destroys the 'passive fallacy'; the intuition of freedom returns like the circulation returning to an arm that has 'gone dead.' With the destruction of the 'passive fallacy' vanishes the idea that nothing is worth doing. It is, so to speak, a tangible reward, a mental holiday that excites the appetite for further similar experiences, as well as the perception that they are entirely a matter of free will. Alcoholism is based on a misconception – not dissimilar to that which produces sadism and other forms of sexual perversion; it is a failure to recognise that the passive attitude towards pleasure is indissolubly connected with the law of diminishing returns. The peak experience destroys this misconception in those intelligent enough to grasp its significance. (I am assuming that the successful cures were all accomplished with the 'Lost Weekend' type of drunk.) Hence the cure.

But what is perhaps most exciting about this experiment is the possibility of its development into a general method. If what characterises the drunk is his unawareness of his freedom, then all human beings are drunks, even the greatest. Certain men of genius excite our respect because they succeed in preserving a high degree of freedom thoughout their creative lives. Too many men of talent make a great initial effort and transform themselves into creative personalities, and then simply allow the new personality to ossify until it becomes as much a prison as the old one. Ernest Hemingway is a clear example; he becomes increasingly a caricature of himself as he gets older. But it is not difficult to think of examples, since, regrettably, most men of talent find it difficult to continue to develop. On the other hand, a Beethoven, a Blake, a W. B. Yeats, excites admiration because of a capacity for self-renewal; a certain tough core of the being continues to develop. What is so remarkable is not, perhaps, the capacity to keep on growing, but to keep on doing it consciously and intelligently, with the aid of self-analysis. No one denies Wagner's greatness; but at an early point in his career, he made the familiar romantic mistake of identifying ultimate freedom with death; this means that the development of his art after *Tristan* is completely predictable; it is bound to turn into the overripe, oversweet fruit of *Parsifal*. Yeats, on the other hand, had the strength to reject his early death-romanticism, at the cost of revising all his early ideas about life and about himself, with the result that he went on to become a great poet.

But such development depends upon an unconquerable optimism and faith in life. The great poet or artist is the man who has somehow instinctively mastered the trick of inducing peak experiences; but sooner or later it deserts him – and at this point, he becomes the self-parodist. The difference between the poet in his greatest moments and in his 'everyday' moments is about equivalent to the difference between, let us say, an enthusiastic school teacher and a habitual drunk. What has been lost is the creativity, the sense of freedom.

This is not to suggest that LSD should be generally used to make most people more purposive and to destroy the passive fallacy in us. Continual use of anything becomes a habit, and habit is the opposite of freedom. But there is a possibility that such drugs might be used occasionally as a stimulus to phenomenological self-analysis – to provide, so to speak, the raw material of inner-impulse upon which such analysis could work. Peak experiences are necessary; they re-charge the creative batteries. A psychologically healthy person has, to some extent, mastered the art of inducing peak experiences without the help of drugs.

Phenomenological analysis is an attempt to discover the conscious structure of *any* experiences – the recipe for re-creating them, as it were. If drugs like LSD can help to provide the peak experiences, and phenomenological analysis can help to uncover their structure, the significance of the method may go far beyond its possibilities as a cure for alcoholism. Hadley Cantril points out that all human activity – and therefore creativity – is based upon assumptions, derived from previous experience, as to its success. An army marching into a battle it expects to lose is unlikely to march with any vigour; it is also almost certain to lose. Other factors are obviously involved: strength of numbers and equipment for example; but it is impossible to say how far these count against the assumption of victory or defeat.

Now phenomenology and transactional psychology have demonstrated that most of the assumptions upon which we live – and have our psychological being – are false. *But the question of how far life itself is a success or a defeat depends upon these assumptions.* Is it not likely that the passive fallacy of perception is as influential in determining the degree to which we experience our freedom as a conviction of inevitable defeat would be to an army marching into battle? Our 'spiritual' lives (I use the word for want of a better) are certainly experienced as a continual conflict between the passive fallacy and sudden knowledge of our inalienable freedom. But for practical, everyday purposes, the passive fallacy is inescapable, simply because our perceptions have to be limited for practical purposes. (Aldous Huxley pointed out that if we all lived in a state of mescalin-awareness, there would be no wars, but there would be no civilisation either; the 'blinkers' that keep us from vision are, to some extent, psychologically necessary.) If the passive fallacy could be totally undermined by some phenomenological discipline, the results for human evolution would be unpredictable – but certainly immense, Our 'human condition' (as we grasp it according to the natural standpoint) is determined by the way we act and live, and consequently become known to ourselves. But our actions are determined by our assumptions about their possibility of success. And our assumptions about their possibility of success are determined by our idea of the 'human condition' (as we grasp it according to the natural standpoint). It can be seen that this is a vicious circle, that has been interrupted only spasmodically by minor manifestations of freedom (in the form of works of art, scientific ideas, philosophies). Phenomenological analysis suggests a sudden radical break in the cycle. It can now, perhaps, be seen why I say that the results are unpredictable.

A final note of warning before I attempt to relate some of these observations to my own 'new existentialism.' *Phenomenology is not a philosophy*; it is a philosophical method, a *tool*. It is like an adjustable spanner that can be used for dismantling a refrigerator or a car, or used for hammering in nails, or even for knocking somebody out. A phenomenologist might be an existentialist or a logical positivist or a neo-Hegelian – or a historian, for that matter. If this is kept in mind, it may save some confusion in the ensuing discussion.

Part Two

THE NEW EXISTENTIALISM

CHAPTER ONE

THE MAN IN THE FOG

The first half of this book has been little more than a clearing of the ground. In this second part, I shall try to show that existentialism, far from being a dead philosophy, is in fact the only modern philosophy with a long and clear road of development ahead of it.

The true 'founder' of this new existentialism is Nietzsche, for it was he who announced the advent of a new optimism. But even Nietzsche did not clearly recognise the character of *inevitability* of this optimism.

In an important article about mysticism – to which I shall refer later – William James has occasion to quote a man who had a 'mystical experience' under ether. When one of the doctors made a remark to the other, the patient chuckled, because he felt that they 'believed they saw real things and causes, but they *didn't*. . . . I was where the causes *were* and to see them required no more mental ability than to recognise a colour as blue. . . . The knowledge of how little (the doctors) actually did see, coupled with their evident feeling that they saw all there was, was funny to the last degree. . . . (They) knew as little of the real causes as does the child who, viewing a passing train and noting its revolving wheels, supposes that they, turning of themselves, give to coaches and locomotive their momentum. Or imagine a man seated in a boat, surrounded by dense fog, and out of the fog seeing a flat stone leap from the crest of one wave to another. *If he had always sat thus*, his explanations must be very crude as compared with those of a man whose eyes could pierce fog, and who saw upon the shore the boy skipping stones. In some such way, the remarks of the two physicians seemed to me like the last two "skips" of a stone thrown from my side. . . .'

I have cited this passage here because these two images – of a boy throwing stones through the fog, or a child watching a railway engine and imagining that the movement of the wheels drives the engine – make an excellent starting point for the 'new existentialism.' Within its limited range, there is nothing actually wrong with Sartre's thinking, or with Heidegger's. It simply does not go far enough. They are men sitting in a boat in the fog.

Let us try to see in one clear recognition why the 'old existentialism' is a failure.

The pre-condition for any human effort is a vision of success. Man is never so strong, so enterprising, so endlessly resourceful, as when his aim stands clearly in front of him, to be achieved by a definite number of determined strides. To 'work without hope' is almost a contradiction in terms, for work without hope is work without real drive, without momentum.

Now the basic impulse behind existentialism is optimistic, very much like the impulse behind all science. Existentialism *is* romanticism, and romanticism is the feeling that man is not the mere creature he has always taken himself for. Romanticism began as a tremendous surge of optimism about the stature of man. Its aim – like that of science – was to raise man above the muddled feelings and impulses of his everyday humanity, and to make him a god-like observer of human existence.

Now, if we turn to Sartre and Heidegger, we can instantly *see* why their existentialism is so unsatisfactory. The great trumpet call of optimism no longer sounds. There is no clear road forward. Heidegger concludes that, with the exception of a few great poets, man achieves 'authenticity' only in the face of death. Sartre's analysis of the human situation leads him to feel that there is no 'life purpose' for all men, no absolute values. The only good is the relative one of human welfare; so the only possible way forward lies in commitment to socialist politics. All roads are blocked but this one. Philosophy is now a closed subject, for there is no point in thinking further; we shall only keep returning to the recognition that all roads are blocked but this one.

This is the challenge the 'new existentialism' has to face. Can it again point to a clear, open road along which thought can advance with the optimism of the early romantics?

I shall try to show that this is exactly what it can do. But first I must reiterate the point that I made earlier in this volume. There is, of course, no 'old existentialism' and 'new existentialism'; these terms have to be used only for purposes of exposition. The 'old existentialism' is a failure only because it cannot penetrate *far enough* into the fog that surrounds the man in the boat. It is 'negative' only through certain errors of judgement. Once we have succeeded in grasping the essence of the 'new existentialism', the fog lifts, and this false distinction between the 'old' and the 'new' vanishes. New vistas appear, and things can suddenly be seen in perspective.

Let us begin by trying to see the exact size and outline of the problem of a 'new existentialism.' *The central problem of existentialism is man's contingency*; and in its most extreme form, this is expressed by William James in the passage about the idiot, and his reflection 'If the hour should strike for me as it struck for him, nothing could save me. . . .' As it happens, it is logically impossible to deny that we do not know whether we shall 'breathe out the very breath we now breathe in.' Consequently, if we are sticking to 'hard facts,' Omar Khayyam is in a far sounder position than Sartre as an existential thinker. Sartre says we know nothing except that men need bread and justice. Omar Khayyam replies that we know nothing except that politicians and philosophers die like animals, so we had better 'fill the cup' and enjoy the present.

Let us confront the 'basic facts.' Men die, and they are subject to chance. These 'facts' are enough to negate all the talks about 'absolute truth,' the indomitable spirit of man, and so on.

From Comte onward, all materialist philosophers have made the same point: that man has invented the 'illusion of central position' – God, religion, the 'human spirit' – to conceal from himself his own fundamental contingency. It certainly requires no great mental effort to see how the Christian heaven – where sins are punished and virtues are rewarded – came into existence. Religion is man's attempt to escape his contingency.

Good. But does this mean that the only ultimate choice for the philosopher lies between Omar Khayyam and the Christian church? (This is certainly the reason that so many 'intellectuals' of the twentieth-century became Christians.) The obstacle that blocks the road of the 'old existentialism' is human contingency. Well, human beings *are* contingent. They die, and they are subject to chance. So how *can* a new existentialism be possible? Unless, that is, it devotes itself to the absurd proposition that human beings do not die and are not subject to accident. But even Bernard Shaw, who believed that there is no ultimate reason why death should not be overcome, still makes his 'Ancients' in *Back to Methuselah* subject to accident.

But this is an attempt to scale the mountain up its steepest face. Let us abandon this question for the moment – while bearing it in mind – and try attacking from another angle.

Contingency is passivity, the opposite of will. All lifeless objects are wholly subject to contingency. A man's experience of contingency is the experience of suddenly feeling himself a mere object (as in that passage in Eliot's *Cocktail Party* about tripping on the stairs and suddenly feeling oneself at the mercy of a flight of stairs).

In that case, it seems slightly absurd that phenomenology preceded Heidegger and Sartre. It should have been discovered later; for it is, to some extent, a denial of the contingency they emphasise. Man takes it for granted that his consciousness is a *passive* observer of the world; phenomenology points out that his consciousness is intentional. I have already tried to show how Sartre, in his attempt to purify phenomenology of the 'transcendental ego,' actually reduced intentionality to a completely negative concept. Sartre was attempting to prove Hume's position: that there is no 'essential you' – that 'you' are the summary of all your moods and memories. But what is the point of showing that consciousness is 'intentional' if you then proceed to prove that the intention is not an intention at all, but a natural law, like water flowing downhill?

This is the first step towards the new existentialism: to recognise that consciousness *is* intentional. The most basic mistake of both Sartre and Heidegger was to misinterpret this intentionality, and consequently to fail to see its implications.

Practical Disciplines

The first *practical* necessity for the existential philosopher is to learn to become constantly aware of the intentionality of all his conscious acts. But as soon as we consider this more closely, we discover that this awareness is only another name for a familiar moral discipline. If we criticise a bad-tempered old man for bullying his family, we are actually criticising him for intentionalising without being aware of it; when he feels annoyance, he promptly blames somebody for it, without recognising that he is only 'projecting' his own feelings. In doing this, he avoids the necessity for self-discipline; it is a form of 'bad faith.' It is equally a form of bad faith if a weakling comes to believe himself constantly in the wrong. In both cases, a certain self-discipline is needed to maintain the balance of objectivity. (And, of course, 'maintaining the balance of objectivity' is a precise definition of the aim of phenomenology.)

In these cases, it is only a matter of becoming aware of an emotional intentionality. It is slightly more difficult – but not very much more – to become constantly aware of other kinds of intentionality: intellectual and perceptual. It is simply a matter of ceasing to accept one's impulses at their surface value, of trying to look at them, as it were, from above. 'Moods' make particularly good material for this kind of analysis, once we have achieved the basic recognition that we are always perceiving the world through the coloured spectacles of some mood or other, and that the world is quite 'other' than we see it; it is 'out there,' independent, indifferent to our moods.

What is important is to develop a continual awareness

of the workings of 'intentionality' that becomes an automatic part of our mental make-up. Anyone who took the trouble could compile a textbook of methods for developing such awareness; for as soon as we begin to look for them, everyday life provides endless examples. Any intelligent person practises an intellectual kind of phenomenology as a matter of course – for example, when reading the political news in various newspapers, or listening to speeches by members of opposed political parties: it is simply an attempt to make allowances for the prejudices involved. Sex is an admirable field for the practice of this kind of analysis. Every person of intelligence has been struck by the fact that sexual experience has a strong element of 'confidence trickery' in it: here the image of a man in a boat surrounded by fog goes to the heart of the matter. Sex is all immediacy; its stream seems to flow powerfully and meaningfully; caught up in that stream, one has a feeling of its irresistible *logic*. Then, the experience over, the logic vanishes – or seems to; it is like a speech heard in a dream that seems to be gibberish when you wake up.

There are also the purely physical disciplines I have already mentioned: the illusions of the transactionists, the Müller-Lyer effect, and so on. If you stare at your feet through the wide end of a pair of powerful binoculars, you will find it impossible to walk a straight line, because your feet seem so distant. But you do not normally need to look at your feet to walk in a straight line. Here is a proof that perception is *not* passive; in this case, it gets between your feet and trips you up.

The aim of all these disciplines is to teach us that consciousness is not passive. It only looks passive, like a sweet-faced and kindly old lady, who on investigation turns out to be a writer of poison-pen letters. To become aware of the continual intentionality of consciousness is to produce a change in consciousness of exactly the kind produced by 'mind changing' drugs. It is true that mescalin, lysergic acid and the rest produce far deeper insights; but at this stage they are useless, since we cannot verbalise their content. The change in consciousness produced by phenomenological disciplines may be less profound, but it is permanent, and susceptible to analysis. When Shaw remarked: 'Our minds are nothing but this knowledge of ourselves; and he who adds a jot to such knowledge creates new mind as surely as any woman creates new men,' he had made a statement in total accord with the findings of phenomenology.

Here, then, is the first and most important objection to the 'old existentialism.' *We cannot talk about contingency until we are in full possession of the facts about the intentionality of consciousness.* For what is subject to contingency is the 'false self,' the idea of ourselves built upon the fallacy of passive perception. Freud's example of the man who forgets his umbrella will clarify this point. We might say of such a man 'He is the victim of his absent-mindedness' (the word 'victim' being almost a synonym for contingency); Freud points out that the absent-mindedness is intentional; hence he is not a victim, and the appearance of contingency is a false one.

I might here risk an over-simplification to attempt to show what is at issue. Every man is a Jekyll and Hyde; a Jekyll of 'passive consciousness,' a Hyde of intentionality. The aim of phenomenological discipline is to destroy the duality, to unite Jekyll and Hyde. The misleading nature of this analogy lies in its implication that Jekyll and Hyde are more or less equal. They are not. Jekyll is a dwarf; Hyde a giant.

CHAPTER TWO

THE EXTENSION OF CONSCIOUSNESS

We are now in a position to go to the heart of the 'new existentialism.' A convenient starting point is the article by William James, *A Suggestion about Mysticism.*[1]

James's suggestion is simply 'that the states of mystical intuition may be only very sudden and great extensions of the ordinary "field of consciousness".' This is in line with an earlier remark (in The *Varieties of Religious Experience*) to the effect that the exaltation produced by alcohol is of the same fundamental nature as mystical experience.

James contends that our field of consciousness is ordinarily narrow (and he uses the image of the man in the boat surrounded by fog to make his meaning clear). At certain moments, 'the present coalesces . . . with ranges of the remote quite out of its reach under ordinary circumstances.' He offers an example from his own experience.

'In each of the three like cases, the experience broke in abruptly upon a perfectly commonplace situation and lasted perhaps less than two minutes. In one instance, I was engaged in conversation, but I doubt whether the interlocutor noticed my abstraction. What happened each time was that I seemed

1. Written shortly before James's death, and printed in *The Journal of Philosophy, Psychology and Scientific Methods,* 1910. Reprinted in *The Psychedelic Review,* No. 5 (1965).

all at once to be reminded of a past experience; and this reminiscence, ere I could conceive or name it distinctly, developed into something further that belonged with it, this in turn into something further still, and so on, until the process faded out, leaving me amazed at the sudden vision of increasing ranges of distant facts of which I could give no articulate account. The mode of consciousness was perceptual, not conceptual – the field expanding so fast that there seemed no time for conception or identification to get in its work. There was a strongly exciting sense that my knowledge of past (or present?) reality was enlarging pulse by pulse, *but so rapidly that my intellectual processes could not keep up the pace.* (My italics.) The *content* was thus entirely lost to introspection – it sank into the limbo into which dreams vanish as we gradually awake. The feeling – I won't call it belief – that I had had a sudden *opening*, had seen through a window, as it were, into distant realities that incomprehensibly belonged with my own life, was so acute that I cannot shake it off today.'

If James had lived another three years, to read Proust's *Swann's Way*, he would instantly have recognised Proust's 'mystical' sensation on tasting the tisane as identical with his own.

James suggests that all mystical experiences are of this nature – although perhaps more violent and extreme. If so, then it is clear that there is no real difference between mystical experience and aesthetic experience. Music and poetry produce exactly this effect – of the fog lifting, and the sudden vision of 'increasing ranges of distant facts' standing up like mountains.

We begin to see the nature of the problem. Human consciousness is narrow, a wedge of light moving through time, creating a perpetual present. The past slips into the darkness, becoming unreal. So it is natural that our notion of 'real' should be tied up with the present. Dr Johnson kicked a stone to refute Berkeley's proposition that matter is unreal; G. E. Moore produced his watch when someone said that time is unreal. The solid present is our criterion of reality. And so it should be. But its narrowness adds a strong element of unreliability to the 'present' as a standard of reality, for it tells us that the past is unreal. It is a common feature of all mystical experiences that they seem to be *more real* than the 'everyday world.' This is because they *reach further*.

And *this* is the confusion that has been built into the foundations of Sartre's philosophy; he keeps appealing to the present as his standard of reality. This can be seen far more clearly in his trilogy of novels than in the philosophical books (where it tends to get concealed by the technical jargon). The world of *Les Chemins de la Liberté* is a world surrounded by fog; there is never the slightest glimpse of the 'increasing ranges of distant facts.' What Sartre presents as the 'reality' of the human situation is only a claustrophobic *present* reality, with no vision of horizons or of real causes.

This glimpse of distant ranges is the fundamental poetic experience. It is what Wordsworth meant by 'other modes of being.' For some reason, human beings are squeezed into a narrow, tight cell of the present; and, as Eliot points out, 'we each think of the key, each in his prison.'

The question that has troubled every poet – and everyone who has experienced this extension of ordinary consciousness – can now be clearly expressed. *Why are we forced to live in this depressing slum of consciousness when our perceptions are perfectly capable of grasping the wider horizons?*

The obvious answer was suggested by Aldous Huxley in *Doors of Perception*: that if we lived all the time in this broader state of consciousness, we would become too lazy to confront the problems of everyday life. This is a depressing notion. It seems that human beings are bound to live like blinkered horses to avoid becoming extinct; the blinkering acts as a protection. Our boredom and dissatisfaction spur us to the effort of building civilisation.

This sounds plausible enough; but when closely examined, certain flaws become apparent. Vision is a far more powerful stimulus than boredom. In fact, everything that human beings have achieved has been achieved through sudden glimpses of the 'ranges of distant facts.' What was Newton's science but a vision of distant facts? The reason that most visionaries do nothing about their visions is the one given by William James – that the intellectual processes cannot grasp the enlarged reality, and so can make little use of it. It is like a man who is lost in some strange country, and who climbs a high mountain to find out where he is. Unless he has a pencil and some paper with him, so that he can make a map, his vision will be useless, for he will forget most of what he has seen by the time he descends to the valley again.

But there is undoubtedly a problem that is analogous to the one Huxley mentioned. James said that his 'vision' simply took in a wider horizon of 'facts' than usual, and that the effect was a sense of exhilaration. But if we were perpetually aware of such a wide horizon of facts, the effect, for most people, would be disastrous. The whole idea of intentionality means that it is not the 'facts' that matter so much as our interpretation of them. Philosophers are men who are concerned with a wider horizon of fact than the average man, and the history of philosophy has ten pessimists to every optimist. That is to say that, given a wide horizon of facts, human beings are inclined to choose the gloomy interpretation. The more facts there are, the gloomier they are inclined to be. Under the circumstances, it may be as well that most of us are 'blinkered.'

The reason for this is obvious enough to anyone who has grasped the concept of intentionality. Human beings possess a great maelstrom of subconscious energy. Luckily, most of this energy is not available to the 'Jekyll' self. It would be disastrous if it were, like giving a child an atomic bomb to play with. For the delusions of passive consciousness make man particularly susceptible to pessimism: that is to say, to 'intentionalising' his perceptions so that they take on a negative flavour. (This concept would have been extremely difficult to grasp fifty years ago; since then, psychoanalysis has taught us that negative subconscious energies can produce the most devastating effects.)

The same point has been made repeatedly by those who have taken mescalin or other mind-changing drugs. Under mescalin, Huxley was asked if he could see where madness lies, and he replied with an emphatic affirmative. 'If you started the wrong way, everything that happened would be proof of the conspiracy against you. . . . If one began with fear and hate as the major premise, one would have to go on to the conclusion.' Mescalin widens the horizons; or, to put it another way, endows the imagination with a tremendous magnifying power. If one's choice of the' facts' were negative, the imagination would magnify them until they became mind-destroying. All of these experiences of wider consciousness can lead to heaven or hell. Given the human tendency to negative-intentionalising, it would mainly lead to hell.

The reason for introducing the word 'imagination' may not be at once apparent. This is because the word 'imagination' suffers from the same ambiguity as 'reality.' If we are speaking of the narrow 'present reality,' then imagination means no more than the ability to escape into a realm of unreality. But as soon as we think in terms of

James's other 'reality' – the 'ranges of distant fact' – this definition becomes inadequate, for these wider ranges of reality are precisely the realms into which imagination was trying to escape. To perceive a distant reality as real is the function of imagination. The words 'perception' and 'imagination' become interchangeable on this level.

The whole point of phenomenology is that there is no sharp dividing line between perception and imagination. The dividing line only applies when we think of perception as passive and imagination as active. As soon as we realise that perception is active, the old dichotomy vanishes.

All this should make it clear, then, why, at this stage in our evolution, it would not be desirable for human beings to have access to 'wider states of consciousness.' This is the objection to Aldous Huxley's suggestion that mescalin should be made as easily available as alcohol or tobacco. It is necessary first of all for human beings to achieve a phenomenological discipline that enables them to recognise how far pessimism is intentional. To give mescalin to the average westerner – with his tendency to neurosis and anxiety – would be like handing a revolver to a man with suicidal tendencies. The only 'safe' way to an enlargement of consciousness is through phenomenological discipline.

It is no accident that the first major work of existential philosophy in the twentieth-century was Jasper's *General Psychopathology*. For, from what has been said above, it should be clear that questions of mental sickness belong to philosophy as much as to psychology.

When William James described his experience of 'abject terror' at the sight of the idiot, he added: 'I awoke morning after morning with a horrible dread in the pit of my stomach, *and with a sense of the insecurity of life that I never knew before*. . . . [My italics.] I remember wondering how other people could live, how I myself ever lived, so unconscious of that pit of insecurity beneath the surface of life. My mother in particular, a very cheerful person, seemed to me a perfect paradox in her unconsciousness of danger. . . .' (*Varieties of Religious Experience*, p. 158)[1].

1. I append here the full text of James's description:
'Whilst in this state of philosophic pessimism and general depression of spirits about my prospects, I went one evening into a dressing room in the twilight to procure some article that was there; when suddenly there fell upon me without any warning, just as if it came out of the darkness, a horrible fear of my own existence. Simultaneously there arose in my mind the image of an epileptic patient whom I had seen in the asylum, a black-haired youth with greenish skin, entirely idiotic, who used to sit all day on one of the benches, or rather shelves against the wall, with his knees drawn up against his chin, and the coarse grey undershirt, which was his only garment, drawn over them inclosing his entire figure. He sat there like a sort of sculptured Egyptian cat or Peruvian mummy, moving nothing but his black eyes, and looking absolutely non-human. This image and my fear entered into a species of combination with each other. *That shape am I*, I felt, potentially. Nothing that I possess can defend me against that fate, if the hour for it should strike for me as it struck for him. There was such a horror of him, and such a perception of my own merely momentary discrepancy from him, that it was as if something hitherto solid within my breast gave way entirely, and I became a mass of quivering fear. After this the universe was changed for me altogether. I awoke morning after morning with a horrible dread at the pit of my stomach, and with a sense of the insecurity of life that I never knew before, and that I have never felt since. It was like a revelation; and although the immediate feelings passed away, the experience has made me sympathetic with the morbid feelings of others ever since. It gradually faded, but for months I was unable to go out into the dark alone.

In general, I dreaded to be left alone. I remember wondering how other people could live, how I myself had ever lived, so unconscious of this pit of insecurity beneath the surface of life. My mother in particular, a very cheerful person, seemed to me a perfect paradox in her unconsciousness of danger, which you may well believe I was very careful not to disturb by revelations of my own state of mind. I have always thought that this experience of melancholia of mine had a religious bearing.'

This is the reason that mescalin can be so dangerous. It may plunge the mind into a nightmare, but *a nightmare from which it is impossible to awake*, because it is actually a preception of a *deeper* reality than that of our everyday lives. It is true that the nightmare is 'intentional,' but since the sufferer does not know it is intentional, this can be no comfort. (The *basic* experience of James's nightmare was identical with that of his glimpse of 'distant horizons' the difference was that in the case of the 'vastation,' he was, as he explains, 'in a state of philosophic pessimism and general depression of spirits about my prospects,' and therefore already inclined to 'intentionalise' negatively.)

To recapitulate: the mind does not *perceive* facts. Perception is an act of *selecting a certain set of facts*, in accordance, so to speak, with one's mood. Our life is a continual act of choice, since perception is an act of choice.

This enables us to state the outlook on human existence that is fundamental to the 'new existentialism.'

Knowledge and power can be dangerous until one knows how to control them. One does not give a child a loaded revolver. For the same reason, no one accuses a parent of dishonesty for telling a child that Santa Claus delivers the Christmas presents. We realise that a child's world needs to be 'protected' – to be narrow and comfortable and artificial, until the child itself feels the curiosity to explore beyond its walls. It would serve no useful purpose to take away *Red Riding Hood* and *Cinderella*, and substitute picture books about Belsen and Hiroshima.

'Walls' are an important condition of human development, and they serve a very positive function. We know that a child's picture book presents a false and oversimplified image of human existence; but it also stimulates the imagination and strengthens the mind. Human beings need a centre of security from which to make forays into the outer-chaos.

This is the reason that human vision is limited. It is limited by an unconscious act of intentionality. We do not want to see too far. We deliberately build 'walls' to protect ourselves.

But here an absurdity arises. The psychological 'blinkers' that are designed to protect our energy and vitality may have the opposite effect. Too much security becomes boredom, and boredom leads to a decline in vitality. Man has surrounded himself by walls, and has built his narrow 'human world' as a centre of security; but the security has begun to stifle him.

This is the main lesson to be learned from the literature of the nineteenth century. Quite suddenly, there appears a subject that no earlier century had touched upon: boredom.

Boredom is the essence of the problem that Goethe propounded in *Faust*. Faust is a man who has devoted his life to the search for knowledge, feeling that knowledge will eventually turn men into gods. In middle life, the great enthusiasm has evaporated. He now 'knows' more than any of his colleagues, but he doesn't feel in the least god-like. This leads him to believe that knowledge is an illusion, that 'we can know nothing.' He has fallen into a total relativism. But why has knowledge failed him? Because, in spite of his urge to explore the universe, he is still trapped in the narrow, boring present. His intellect alone cannot carry his vision outward towards the horizons of distant facts. He remains the man in a boat surrounded by fog. And he recognises that the nets of the intellect are too wide to catch the more important kinds of knowledge. Man uses his intellect to prevent his experience from escaping him. But the essence of the experience escapes, all the same. Conscious memory only preserves a thin, faded photograph of the experience – of the pleasures of childhood, for example. Faust makes this discovery when the Easter bells ring and suddenly evoke the essence of his childhood.

This episode of the Easter bells is of symbolic importance. Faust was on the point of committing suicide when the bells rang; he has examined his life and decided it is not worth living. He has certainly examined it to the best of his ability *with his intellect.* What the bells teach him is that, in this matter, the intellect is a false guide. It is the fallacy of all intellectuals to believe that intellect can grasp life. It cannot, because it works in terms of symbols and language. There is another factor involved: consciousness. If the flame of consciousness is low, a symbol has no power to evoke reality, and intellect is helpless.

But still, the episode of the Easter bells is a great affirmation. Their effect on Faust is the same as the effect of mescalin on Aldous Huxley: to reveal the world in its untouched, pristine beauty. So it is no cause for pessimism that the intellect cannot grasp life. The Easter bells declare that the source of all pessimism is the limitations of human consciousness. But what does that matter? We possess senses and emotions. 'Five windows light the caverned man,' as Blake says, and if these windows are cleaned, the result is that everything is seen as it really is – infinite. Faust's discipline has simply been too narrow. Goethe recognised this when he made Faust turn back to the world of emotions and sensations. The Easter bells are a symbol of the 'beyond,' the assertion of the *real existence* of a world of beauty and intensity beyond our narrow human consciousness.

This sounds a commonplace enough assertion, but it is of crucial importance. For this belief is precisely what is missing from the world of the 'old existentialism.' (The later Heidegger becomes altogether more positive, but this is no place to speak of that.) The 'philosophical equation', as propounded by Sartre or Camus, insists on sticking to 'this world,' as revealed to us through our limited consciousness. On such a basis, it was inevitable that they should end in a *cul de sac*.

But if the way out of the *cul de sac* lies in the recognition of the *real existence* of this world of beauty and intensity beyond everyday consciousness, what then? The next stage for a 'new existentialism' should be to propound some infallible intellectual discipline for reaching this world. Phenomenological analysis has confirmed what Blake asserted a century earlier: that our senses are liars. This is, of course, an absurd way of putting it. Our senses are not liars; they do not try to convince us that our narrow and limited vision is universally true. It is we who misinterpret their evidence and deceive ourselves with it. The remedy is to make phenomenological analysis a second nature, and to make it a fundamental premise of our lives that the world of beauty and intensity has a real existence.

I have spoken at length of Faust, but I might equally well have spoken of Oblomov, or the heroes of Dostoevsky (particularly Kirilov and Stavrogin in *Devils*), or the heroes of Chekhov. (Because of its provincialism, Russia produced an extremely rich crop of the 'literature of boredom' in the nineteenth century.) All these figures make ideal illustrations of what one writer has called 'the great mystery of human boredom.' But they all illustrate the same point: that in the past century and a half, man's protective 'walls' have become a source of potential danger. They threaten to suffocate him.

It should now be clear that, if the reasoning in this chapter is correct, then the 'old existentialism' is limited and self-contradictory. In that case, what sort of philosophical edifice can be built on these foundations? But before turning to this question, let us look a little more closely at the problem of 'limited consciousness.'

CHAPTER THREE

INSIDE THE DARK ROOM

The 'great mystery of human boredom' became a subject of scientific investigation fairly recently. People with monotonous jobs – long-distance lorry drivers, radar workers, and so on – often experience sensory delusions – see phantom hitch-hikers or a radar pip that isn't really there. At Princeton University, a research unit was set up to investigate the effects of 'sensory deprivation' (often shortened to S.D.). In his book on mescalin, Aldous Huxley had observed that human beings who are immersed in a bath of lukewarm water in a dark room begin to experience hallucinations. The Princeton research team created a dark room into which no sound could penetrate, and provided it with a huge bed, a supply of food, and a chemical toilet. Subjects were asked to remain in this room for as many days as possible.

The results of these tests[1] give us a great deal of material for reflection on the question of 'intentionality.'

Three days was the limit that most people could bear, although many claimed that they could have stayed longer. Certain subjects pressed the 'panic button' after less than half a day. (Oddly enough, it was impossible to foretell in advance who would do this.) The more intelligent subjects found it far more oppressive than the less intelligent

1. See *Inside the Black Room* by Jack Vernon, Souvenir Press.

ones. Mostly, the subjects slept for the first twelve hours or so – it often extended as far as twenty-four hours. After that, confinement became steadily more oppressive. It was discovered that subjects became more susceptible to propaganda – played on a tape – after only twenty-four hours in the 'dark room.'

These effects, perhaps, are predictable. Gurdjieff once declared that sensory stimuli are as necessary to people as food and drink – in fact, *are* a kind of food and drink. But some of the effects were less so. People with bad colds were used as subjects; the colds disappeared completely in two days. Two men suffering from ivy poisoning on the hands and forearms were admitted, and their hands were covered with gloves so that they could not scratch. (This was accidental; the research team were unaware of the ivy poisoning.) One might have predicted that forty-eight hours in a dark room, forbidden to scratch the itchy places, would have been hell. In fact, they endured it very well, and the ivy poisoning disappeared in two days. As with the colds, this was a far shorter time than would normally have been taken. Chain smokers discovered that they felt no desire to smoke in their 'solitary confinement.'

As with mescalin, the effects seem strangely contradictory. But in the light of what was said in the last chapter, they are easy enough to explain; they become another illustration of the working of intentionality. To understand the panic, we have only to think of what happens if we are bored, and the foot begins to itch. We scratch it, and the itch removes itself to some other place . . . and so on.[1] Or of what happens when we feel sick, and manage

1. An acquaintance told me a story that makes an ideal illustration. When he was a child of about six, the chimney of their sitting-room caught fire. His father removed a metal plate halfway up the chimney, and he was fascinated to see the burning soot. At this point, his younger brother became panic-stricken in case the

to dissipate the sickness by thinking about other things; in this case, it is obvious that thinking about the sickness deepens and prolongs it, whereas it would disappear if we could take sufficient interest in something else. In the same way, the subject in the dark room feels boredom and a vague sense of discomfort. Having nothing to distract his attention from it, the full battery of his powers of 'intentionality' are turned on it, magnifying it tenfold, with a result that can turn into panic.

On the other hand, if we have a cold or some other physical ailment, the sheer distractions of everyday life prevent us from turning the full battery of intentionality on it – in this case, to cure it. The dark room releases these inner powers, which 'melt' the ailment like the sun on ice.

(In the light of these observations, some of the 'absurd' claims made by Christian Scientists begin to seem less unreasonable. They claim that by a certain act of 'faith,' analogous to the Zen addict's flash of enlightenment, an illness can be instantly dissipated. The 'act of faith' may be no more than a way of concentrating these powers of intentionality.)

Let us look further into the implications of these ideas.

---

house caught fire, and began to cry. He comforted his brother and told him that he was being silly. But as soon as his brother's fears vanished, he began to wonder what would happen if the upper rooms caught fire, and became panic-stricken. He tried to explain this to me by saying: 'I didn't really *believe* the upstairs rooms would catch fire; but when my brother stopped crying, I experienced a sense of anti-climax, and began to imagine what it would be like. Then my imagination seemed to run away with me, and I couldn't control the panic.' He also mentioned that, when he was a child, he was once warned never to think of ghosts in the dark, because it would make one appear; the result was that whenever he was alone in the dark, he felt a terrible compulsion to think of ghosts, that would become stronger as he became more frightened.

No one, of course, is claiming that they are entirely new. Pascal's *Pensées* deals with man's perpetual need for distraction, his fear of being alone. As to man's untapped inner resources, explorers have often noticed man's extraordinary powers of endurance under crisis. And Don Juan in *Man and Superman* points out that a man with a passionately held belief is almost invincible, while the strongest man becomes a moral coward without a deeply held conviction.

But the dark room experiments, like the researches of the transactionists and existential psychologists, enable us to relate these observations to a larger picture of the human psyche. It seems clear that man possesses enormous powers which he prefers not to use, because their use is at present dangerous. 'Ordinary consciousness' – which human beings refer to simply as 'consciousness' and accept as an absolute – is no more than a kind of safety measure. Man has, so to speak, voluntarily cut himself off from the main power house of his energy, and restricted himself to a pocket generator, which is sufficient to provide energy for the narrow world inside the 'walls.'

But in cutting himself off from the outer reaches of consciousness, he has also cut himself off from a sense of purpose. He relies upon a certain instinctive purpose that remains 'sub-threshold.' But the more intelligent and self-critical he becomes, the more he is cut off from this instinctive sense of life-purpose. A time arrives, therefore, when he 'wakes up' to a sense of the total absurdity of his position in the restricted world of ordinary consciousness. This is the moment that he asks a question that seems meaningless to less intelligent types: Who am I? Tolstoy's story *Diary of a Madman* dramatises such an awakening. His central character, on a business trip that takes him far from home, wakes in the middle of the night to feel suddenly the absurdity of accepting our lives without question – and the fear that the whole thing may be some awful mistake, or some cunning trap. (And a parable of Gurdjieff's makes the point even clearer, for he compares human beings to hypnotised sheep who are being fattened for the butcher.) H. G. Wells had such an awakening at the end of his life, which he expressed in the pessimistic *Mind at the End of Its Tether*. James's experience with the idiot was of the same type; so was the experience that Sartre described in *Nausea*.

We can now see why Faust's solution to this problem was the wrong one (as was T. E. Lawrence's a century later). He tried to go backwards, to *sink* to a more instinctive level. (In the same way, Lawrence said he envied a soldier with his girl, or a man stroking a dog.) Clearly, this is no solution. The solution is to regain the sense of purpose through a deepening of consciousness – which can be achieved by phenomenological analysis. Mescalin, of course, will do it with far less effort, as Huxley showed; but the disadvantage is that when 'ordinary consciousness' returns, the *meaning content* of the mescalin vision is forgotten. Phenomenological discipline may be a far harder path, but it is surer.

It might well be objected that in all this talk about mescalin and consciousness, we have left the realm of philosophy and moved into that of psychology. (In the same way, certain phenomenologists accuse the later Husserl of ceasing to be a philosopher and moving into realms midway between psychology and religious speculation.) I hope that later chapters will show that this idea is based on a misunderstanding. But in the meantime, it might be pointed out that both Sartre and Heidegger have been concerned with these same questions – although in a less specific way. It must not be forgotten that we are not talking about mystical experience, or even (necessarily) about experience under drugs. James's glimpse of 'horizons of distant facts' occurred in the course of an ordinary conversation. The reason that we find it difficult to 'emphasise' our way easily into such an experience is that we cannot grasp the idea that *at this very moment*, we are in the position of the man in the boat surrounded by fog. This ordinary world *looks* sane enough. One and one make two; effects follow causes. We cannot believe that our vision is restricted, and that we no more see causes than the man sees the boy skimming stones on the water. It takes a rather unpleasant kind of awakening to make us realise that this world is 'absurd.' (Absurdity, of course, means to be without causes – like the grin of the Cheshire cat that remains in the air after the rest of the cat has gone; when the man in the boat realises that the stones cannot be skipping over the waves of their own volition, he has awakened to the absurdity of his situation.)

Heidegger – as has already been noted – was centrally concerned about our 'forgetfulness of existence,' which he regards as the cause of the crisis of the modern world. It is, of course, synonymous with boredom or over-familiarity. James's experience of 'horizons of distant fact' was the opposite of such forgetfulness; everything becomes more real. Both Heidegger and Sartre had the same suggestion to make about 'forgetfulness of existence' (which is also a loss of freedom): to face the fact of death. To face death reawakens man to the horizons of possibility beyond the present. Crisis or danger can have the same effect ('freedom is terror' says Sartre). But it can be seen that these suggestions are essentially negative (and Sartre's advocacy of 'terror' in the *Critique of Dialectical Reason* has an almost juvenile flavour).

All this should make it clear that the 'new existentialism'

is no more than an attempt to develop the positive possibilities that are already inherent in the 'old existentialism,' which, for the reasons examined in the first part of this book, was unable to advance beyond the negative stage.

The 'new existentialism,' then, is founded upon a dual recognition: (a) that 'ordinary' human consciousness is restricted, and (b) that this restriction is, in a certain sense, *voluntary*. This latter point is easy enough to grasp if we consider what happens when we try to concentrate on something in unfavourable surroundings – let us say, writing a letter in a roomful of children. If we are successful, we voluntarily exclude consciousness of the noise of children – although, under different circumstances, we might find it agreeable. In fact, we might find ourselves writing a letter sitting at the side of a stream on a sunny day, where all the sights and sounds are entirely agreeable; nevertheless, it is more important to concentrate. This kind of 'exclusion' has become a habit with human beings.

This restriction of consciousness gives rise to a paradox which I have elsewhere called 'the St. Neot Margin' (a purely personal label) or 'the indifference threshold.' A man who has got into the habit of concentrating in the midst of distractions may find that his 'exclusion' of his surroundings has become a *habit*. We have all had the experience of becoming mentally exhausted while trying to finish a book 'in one sitting,' and finding ourselves quite unable to relax or enjoy anything for a few hours afterwards. Our 'excluding' faculty has got jammed, and we continue to look at things with indifference. It is, in fact, a form of 'forgetfulness of existence.'

Once we are in this state of 'indifference,' it is extremely difficult for pleasures to get through to us. On the other hand, the prospect of pain or inconvenience administers a jar to the 'excluding faculty' and unjams it. I have called this state in which we can be stimulated by pain (or inconvenience) but not by pleasure 'the indifference threshold.'

When we think about it, we discover that the 'indifference threshold' plays a profoundly important part in conscious life. One needs to be very little of a philosopher to notice it. A man spends his life struggling to achieve something; as soon as he achieves it, he is bored. Man is never so deeply aware of his need for freedom as when he is in chains. Strike off the chains, and his vision of freedom becomes altogether dimmer. (Sartre remarked that he never felt so free as during the war, working in the Resistance, under the constant threat of danger.)

All this is caught in the old nursery tale of the old woman in the vinegar bottle. A passing fairy heard her complaining that she was too cramped, and transformed the vinegar bottle into a cottage. Passing by a month later, she stopped to see how the old lady was faring, and found her complaining that she was still too cramped. She transformed the cottage into a small house . . . And so on until the fairy has transformed the vinegar bottle into a palace; and *still* the old woman finds something to complain about. So the fairy turns the palace back into a vinegar bottle.

The reverse side of the coin can be found in the story of the Jewish peasant who went to the rabbi to complain that his hut was too small for his increasing family. The rabbi told him to take his cow and goat into the hut as well, and at the end of a week, put them out again; the hut would then seem to be as big as a palace.

The subject of both stories is the *negative* element in the human sense of values. They could be used by a reactionary philosopher to illustrate that it is impossible to make men any happier. But this would be a superficial and facile interpretation. Shaw pointed out that a child has less capacity for freedom than an adult; it becomes bored with a holiday after the first few days. In fact, we *can* mature and gain a more positive capacity for freedom. But freedom itself is a far more complex matter than Rousseau ever realised.

To some extent, the problem is a biological one. As H. G. Wells says, from the beginning of time, animals have been 'up against it.' In order to survive, they had to keep the attention narrow and alert, to concentrate on the business in hand, to be constantly on the lookout for enemies. Man has evolved to his present position by his capacity to narrow his attention, to 'exclude' whatever has nothing to do with the business in hand. This excluding has become a habit, so that when he ceases to strive, he becomes bored. He has built civilisation out of boredom and restlessness. 'Excluding' has become second nature, and he cannot drop it easily. But it is now becoming a considerable problem. Man has the technical resources for creating a world-wide Utopia. It is time for man to evolve to a new level, in which contemplation comes naturally, in which he explores the world of his own being. But the habit of a million years cannot be broken as easily as that.

The biological approach enables us to see the problem with a new clarity. It was H. G. Wells who made the suggestion that man is in the same position as the early amphibians who tried to leave the sea and become land animals. They hated the sea – this must have been the impulse that drove them on to land – but they had only fins and flippers, so that they were incapable of moving properly on land. Wells (in *Experiment in Autobiography*) compares the position of these 'halfway' animals to his own as a writer. The central impulse of his life is to turn inward, to 'create new mind'; he detests the futile interruptions of mere physical existence – feeling, like Axel, that 'as for living, our servants can do that for us.' Even so, the creative intellectual worker is unable to make a definite choice; he remains torn between two worlds.

Wells's evolutionism is shared also by Sir Julian Huxley and Pierre Teilhard de Chardin. In fact, the views expressed in *The Phenomenon of Man* are little more than an elaboration of Wells's position. Everything in Teilhard is based upon this recognition that man is a 'halfway' creature who is stuck uncomfortably between the physical world and the 'country of the mind.' Teilhard calls this latter the 'noösphere,' and the former the 'biosphere.' Man has evolved to a point where he strongly objects to his dependence on the biosphere. He may feel contempt for the café proprietor whose head empties when his café empties; but he knows that he is not really so different from the café owner. He knows that, to a large extent, he is an automaton whose life is spent in 'partial observation of his own automatism' (Eliot's phrase). This is the problem confronted by all romantic – and scientific – idealists. The realms of knowledge seem to promise an increase in power, an escape from human contingency. He imagines his mind ploughing into these new realms like a ship into an unknown sea. He feels his old personality being shed like a snake's skin as he advances. He catches an intuitive vision of 'men like gods,' of a man who is never subject to boredom, for whom the world is endlessly fascinating and beautiful, of endless vistas of new knowledge and new powers. *Above all*, there is this idea of the conquest of boredom. Our lives contain so much boredom and unfulfilment and acceptance of second-best.

But he always reckons without the 'indifference threshold,' the old woman in the vinegar bottle. In due course, there is a disillusioned Faust, feeling that he has traded his youth for fairy gold. The vision of 'men like gods' vanishes. He becomes aware that he is a victim of his 'automatism,' that his body and his psychological habits drag him back to the physical world. We are not strong enough. The world itself is a gigantic 'dark room' that proves that we are too dependent on physical stimuli. The countries of the mind may be vast, but man cannot get a visa to stay there. He can only get a day ticket that forces him to return every night.

It must be understood that all this is not theoretical biology, but straightforward *observation. This* is the problem of the nineteenth-century poets and romantics; this is why there were so many suicides and early deaths. First of all came the vision of man with new powers, new senses to enter into nature, to appreciate the world he has been born into. There were ecstasies and insights and moments of oneness with nature. Then the 'visionary gleam' fled, and the poet found himself back in the 'light of common day.' He was as shattered as a man who is thrown over by the woman he loves. Shelley's *Alastor* is an allegory of the poet who spends his life searching for the vision he has once embraced in a dream – until he dies of despair.

Poetry in the nineteenth century came very close to religious mysticism – in fact, recognised that its quest was identical with that of the mystic. (This is no doubt why so many of the *fin de siécle* poets became converts.) Conversely, a mystic like the Hindu Ramakrishna can be seen as a more successful version of the romantic poet – more successful because he was born into a country and a religious tradition that enabled him to be single-minded about his aim. As a child, Ramakrishna once saw a flight of white cranes flying against a dark thundercloud, and was so overcome with ecstasy that he collapsed in a faint. Later, a suicide attempt brought a sudden vision of 'the divine mother,' and a state of 'samadhi' (mystic ecstasy). All this remains in the romantic-existential tradition. The confrontation with death destroys the 'indifference threshold,' and he experiences a far more powerful version of William James's experience of 'distant ranges of fact.'

Ramakrishna seems to have solved the romantic problem. He can shuttle back and forth freely between the physical world and the world of the spirit; a mere mention of the name of Krishna or Kali is enough to send him into a state of samadhi. And yet the overall impression of his life is unsatisfactory – as it emerges in various biographies – and his death from cancer of the throat only underlines this feeling of ultimate failure. Mysticism, it seems, is no answer.

But what becomes clear from Wells and Teilhard is that *man is a purposive animal.* He is at his best when driven by a purpose. Otherwise, he is strange and paradoxical creature. Most animals are easily contented. Given a full stomach and a sunny day, a lion will rest as contentedly as a cow. No dog or cat behaves like the old woman in the vinegar bottle – or like Alexander the Great, crying for new lands to conquer. But why *did* the old woman in the vinegar bottle behave so badly? It may have been out of sheer feeble-mindedness and lack of self-discipline. But it may also have been because she also experienced the need for some deeper and more purposive mode of existence. Most people do not know themselves well enough to know what they want; but they have a sound instinct about what they don't want. Man is a purposive creature; there is no reason why he should be satisfied with a cottage or a palace.

But *what* purpose? This becomes an increasing problem in the twentieth century, when the intelligent man has become too critical to swallow the religious or political convictions that offer themselves. 'Civilisation cannot survive without a religion,' says Shaw, and one can see his point. He is only saying that man is a purposive creature and that material prosperity and security are no substitute for the sense of purpose. (There is a grim parable by Briussov called *The Republic of the Southern Cross* in which an 'ideal society,' with no material needs – and no idealistic sense of purpose either – explodes into a kind of spontaneous insanity and destroys itself. The story was written before two world wars had underlined the point.)

This problem of purpose is undoubtedly the great question mark that existentialism failed to attack. *This* is why existentialism ended in a *cul de sac*. It is not enough to declare that the answer is universal socialism or universal justice, or that everyone must make his own choice. *What* choice?

It is no evasion to say that the answer is tied up with Faust. For in the year 1800, it must have seemed to many intelligent people that the religion of idealism and human progress was going to replace the old religions of dogma and the supernatural. This new religion of idealism is incarnated in Faust. So what went wrong? What is it that prevents the human spirit from marching 'upward and on,' of becoming god-like through knowledge and poetry and belief in the spirit of man? It was not (we should note) that the religion of progress was too materialistic. The romantics are always talking about God – even atheists like Shelley.

Existentialism groped towards an answer but never reached it. Facing a firing squad, Graham Greene's whisky priest recognised that 'it would have been so easy to be a saint.' Heidegger also recognised that man achieves a glimpse of 'authenticity' in the face of death. What is this except to say that man is inauthentic without a purpose – is, in some fundamental sense, incomplete, like a car without petrol?

One thing is certain. The 'purpose' must be grasped by the visionary intellect. The man in the boat has to learn to see beyond the fog, to escape his involvement in the world of false causes and effects. The purpose cannot be manufactured by some new prophet and made into a rallying cry. Neither does the solution lie in Arnold Toynbee's suggestion of a 'universal religion' made by boiling up Christianity, Hinduism, Mahommedanism and the rest in the same pot. There can be no 'concrete solution' to the problem – that is, no solution that can be immediately applied to the 'man in the street.' But then, this is hardly important. No great discovery was ever made for the benefit of the man in the street. Newton had no idea of inaugurating the industrial revolution when he invented the calculus; Einstein was not thinking about atomic energy when he created the theory of relativity.

All that stands in the way of a solution – and a new phase of development for our civilisation – is the question that Goethe expressed in *Faust*; and which, as we have seen, boils down to the question of the 'indifference threshold,' the 'great mystery of human boredom.' Existentialism has been one long attack on this problem. But, from our point of view, the first real step towards solving it has been taken by the McGill and Princeton research teams into sensory deprivation. For they make it very clear why Faust was unable to continue along the road he started. The scholar poring over his books is suffering from sensory deprivation, which finally becomes so acute that all his enthusiasm vanishes. But this recognition is only the first step towards a solution. It only points to a new problem. Sensory deprivation *can* be combated; it is not an absolute, Faust's original sense of idealistic purpose was proof against it; it took several years for this purpose to become enfeebled.

This may sound like an oversimplification; but that is only because we are not aware of the depth and complexity of this problem of sensory deprivation. We tend to think of it as if it were the same thing as vitamin deficiency. It is not; it is directly connected with the most vital questions of human existence. Raskolnikov, when he thought about the possibility of being executed for murder, reflected that he would prefer to stand on a narrow ledge for all eternity, surrounded by darkness and tempest, rather than die at once. The fear of death has raised his consciousness of freedom to a point where he becomes aware of the absolute value of his existence. The 'indifference threshold' has been completely destroyed; consequently, the thought of sensory deprivation ceases to trouble him. Sensory deprivation, the indifference threshold, and states of 'mystical perception,' are directly connected.

This matter can be expressed more clearly by referring back to Teilhard. Teilhard contended that there is an *absolute* break between man and the lower animals, just as there is between a living creature and a stone. A stone has no freedom at all because it has no life. It is energy without freedom, and could be represented by a straight line which has length but no thickness. All living creatures have a dimension of freedom, and could be symbolised by a square. But all animals are completely dependent on external stimuli; we can say of them (as of the café owner) that their heads empty when there are no stimuli present.

Now it *ought* to be possible to say that man is a 'cube' – that he has yet another dimension of inner freedom, this ability to swim off into the noösphere, to extend his actions into a purely mental sphere. Unfortunately, it would not be true, for the dark-room experiments show us how far man is dependent on external stimuli. The challenges of the mental world are not powerful enough to keep his vitality high. That is to say that *man does not yet exist*. The creature we call man is a halfway house between the animals and the truly human.

This is not as discouraging as it sounds. Shaw says 'The brain will not fail when the will is in earnest.' Show man a problem that obstructs his progress, and he will blast it out of the way by sheer will power. *But until he sees the problem clearly, he is helpless.* It must be stated with such clarity that the full force of human will and intelligence can be brought to bear on it.

Existentialism set out to do this – and failed. It got lost in a labyrinth of its own creating. But now we can see the nature of the obstruction, there is no reason why it should not extricate itself and go on to solve the problem

All that I have said so far is 'foundation work.' In the following chapters, I shall attempt to at least sketch an outline of the building that is to rise on the foundations. It is a question of method.

The major mistake of the nineteenth-century romantics – and it is repeated by existentialism – was to look for a 'practical' solution: religious conversion, political engagement. In *Doktor Faustus*, Mann even nostalgically revives the old idea of selling one's soul to the devil. The idea that philosophy might provide the answer struck them as somehow too cold and uninviting. And yet it becomes increasingly apparent that this is where the answer lies. It is interesting to consider the history of romanticism – the way it has squirmed first one way, then the other, in an attempt to find its solution in some simple realm of action. It begins with Goethe's Faust turning to a love affair, and Schiller's Karl Moor deciding to become a robber. Twenty years more, and total defeat is taken for granted; the poet cannot live in this world; he has to die and hope that he will find his vision on the other side of death. And so we get a long procession of the 'death devoted,' from Novalis to Verlaine. In the new century, a few belated romantics – Mann, Proust, Hesse – attack the problem again. They are actually existentialist philosophers using the novel as a medium for exploring the problems. Proust has an experience that is identical with that of William James, when he tastes a cake dipped in tea, and the 'fog' suddenly lifts, revealing distant horizons of his own life. His long novel is a kind of fictional counterpart of Heidegger's *Sein und Zeit*, and certain passages in it have a psychological penetration comparable to Heidegger[1]. But since Proust's philosophy is basically pessimistic, no final solution can be expected here.

Hesse provides an even more interesting example because he recapitulates the whole history of nineteenth-century romanticism in his work. In early novels like *Peter Camenzind*, the hero is a traveller, hoping to find

1. For example, Marcel's analysis, in *Ombre des Jeunes Filles*, of his reaction to the girl selling coffee on a wayside railway station near Balbec.

his ideal somewhere in the world – like Shelley's Alastor. In *Demian*, the ideal becomes a mystical mother-figure. In *Siddartha* and *Journey to the East*, he toys with eastern religious disciplines and the idea of some mystical brotherhood of adepts that arouses echoes of Madame Blavatsky.

In *Steppenwolf* he states the problem with magnificent clarity – for which reason, this remains his most satisfying novel. Steppenwolf is the bored, middle-aged man who lives alone and spends his days reading and playing gramophone records of Mozart, and toying with the idea of suicide. But in certain moments, he has the experience described by James; the horizons open, and he realises 'how rich was the gallery of my life'; he is reminded 'of Mozart and the stars.' This could not possibly be clearer. *Steppenwolf* is about the indifference threshold, about the 'great mystery of human boredom.' It asks the question: *Why* are the powers of men like Steppenwolf paralysed by this strange mental torpor? Would not man be altogether better off if his consciousness could be permanently extended to these 'distant horizons'? For instead of wasting days in a state of boredom and torpor, he could use his powers to create, to attack the problem of the next stage in human evolution.

But Hesse can find no solution. His last major work, *The Bead Game*, returns to the idea of an order of adepts, a kind of humanistic religion of the future, in which the 'eternal quest' is symbolised in the ritual of the 'bead game.' Instead of becoming a Catholic convert, Hesse has created his own religion; but the result is the same: stagnation.

The problem itself could not be clearer, and the clear statement of a problem is certainly the most important step towards its solution. What now remains is the problem of method, of the tools for attacking it. Newton was able to write the *Principia*, and solve all the age-old problems of astronomy in one sweep, not because he had a better brain than Galileo or Descartes, but because he had stumbled on the right *tool*, the calculus. The main problem for the 'new existentialism' is to create a tool of philosophical analysis like the calculus.

CHAPTER FOUR

LANGUAGE AND VALUES

What we have done is to re-state basic religious issues in a philosophical language. Religion is the belief that this everyday human reality is not the final truth, and that there is another order of reality that is usually inaccessible to human consciousness. But religion is inclined to speak of two 'realities,' two realms of truth, when, in fact, the 'two realities' are only two aspects of the same reality: one seen, as it were, with a microscope, the other with a telescope. For everyday human existence, a microscope is a far more useful instrument than a telescope, since we are dealing with small problems. But we also need the telescope, the over-all glimpse; for this provides us with our motive force, our knowledge of what has to be done. Man's trouble is that he tends to get trapped in the world of the microscope, to lose his sense of purpose among trivialities. His glimpses tend to come accidentally. His problem is to learn how to make them come when they are needed. He is in the position of a man who owns an enormous and complicated machine that is capable of fulfilling all his needs – but with no idea of how to operate it. He does not know where to find the control that operates consciousness.

The necessity is simple: to 'understand the machine.' An engineer faced with such a problem would approach it phenomenologically. That is to say, he would begin by attaching labels to every lever and button on the machine; then he would press them one by one, and write a *description* of what occurred. And, like any scientist, he will exercise the privilege of inventing new words to describe effects for which the old language is inadequate.

Let us examine the nature of language for a moment. Consider the sentence 'Language aims at describing facts.' The word 'aims' is a metaphor; language is not a gun or a bow and arrow. If we said 'Language strives to describe facts,' we would still be inaccurate; it is not language that strives, but the person using it.

So although language is concerned with facts – and the connection between facts – it does not 'stick to facts.' It achieves most of its results by metaphor, by gestures and indications. If we open any book – even a volume of nursery tales – we soon discover that language is not 'tailored to fit reality'; it is mostly a very loose-fitting garment. Language is not accurate, for the most part. A sentence like 'The cat sat on the mat' may be accurate enough; but as soon as we try to express an idea of any complexity, we have to start relying on metaphor and gesture. (By 'gesture,' I mean the word that is not quite accurate, but points in the direction of the meaning it wishes to convey.)

Even this does not describe the complexity of the problem. When I am trying to explain something fairly complex, my 'gestures' rely upon a certain common ground of understanding between myself and the reader. But language itself is an attempt to establish such a common ground. The words 'common ground or understanding' imply a *pattern of facts* that is perceived by both myself and the reader. But since language is concerned with the relations between facts, the 'pattern of facts' should be the *end* product of language. In other words, language should begin, ideally, with a separate word for each separate fact, and then proceed to deal with the relations between the facts. Instead, it has to keep gesturing towards the 'common ground' of facts in order to go forward at all. If the 'common ground' happens to contain misapprehensions about the relation of facts, then these misapprehensions will almost certainly be carried over into the language itself.

Language is at its simplest when it corresponds to simple experiences the most people have in common. From there on, it can be extended to *evoke* experiences that are less common. For example, a man who has travelled to a distant land can reckon to make most of his experiences understood to the people who stayed at home by describing his new experiences in terms of the old common ground. But such a traveller is always aware of the treachery of language, for he knows that his audience will continue to see his adventures in terms of their own limited experience. His audience might live in a temperate climate, so that the word 'sun' evokes thoughts of boating on the river and cricket on the village green; such an audience would find it hard to understand the state of mind of a man crossing the Sahara.

When it is a matter of conveying ideas, the problem becomes far more acute. It is far more difficult to persuade an audience to accompany you on a journey of ideas, since ideas cannot be experienced vicariously, like travel. To understand properly, the reader has to plod over every inch of the road. And here the difference between a limited experience and a wider experience becomes enormous. It is easy enough for a stay-at-home to understand that the Sahara sun might be less pleasant than the sun at Hampton Court; no one declares that this is a paradox, or an example of two different orders of truth about the sun. But mental stay-at-homes find it almost impossible to make the adjustments that would enable them to understand the implications of a bold idea. An obvious example is the difficulty experienced by a layman in trying to understand the theory of relativity. In the same way, a man who had been brought up in some narrow religious tradition, with the notion that an atheist is a monster of evil, will find it quite impossible to grasp the aim of Hegel's philosophy, which is at once religious and agnostic.

Let us consider for a moment how language operates, and how 'new language' comes into existence.

The most straightforward way in which 'new language' makes its appearance is when a 'new object' requires a name. The 'new object' may be genuinely new – a new chemical element, a new species of microbe. But it may be only a variant on something that already exists. The word 'spiv' that came into existence in the nineteen forties describes a particular type of crook. It conjures up an extremely precise picture for the people who have had experience of spivs. To explain the word 'spiv' to a man from some distant country would require a great many words; he would have to be made familiar with the social background that produced spivs.

Now consider the word 'existentialism.' Like 'spiv,' it arose out of a necessity: the necessity for describing a certain *state of things*, a dilemma, that is apparent to anyone with an interest in philosophy or literature. But anyone who has tried to explain existentialism, even to a highly intelligent interlocutor, knows how difficult it can be. Explanations lasting an hour can leave the questioner in a state of 'mystified enlightenment.' There are short cuts; for example, one might begin by describing Leibniz's idea of a 'universal logic' that would enable philosophers to reach any 'truth' by infallible mathematical rules; then point out that such a logical calculus cannot get to grips with certain basic human problems . . . and so on. Unfortunately, such a course would probably leave the questioner with the vague idea that existentialism is somehow tied up with Leibniz and symbolic logic.

But this example makes clear why genuine 'new language' is so difficult to create. It is analogous to building a road into the wilderness. Our ordinary language is definite because it has a *scaffolding* of everyday experience around it, and this scaffolding acts as a co-ordinate system, enabling one to define any point with a certain precision. But to give a new word a definite meaning, one has to erect a system of scaffolding to support it. It is quite a straightforward problem. In the same way, a student of mathematics would find it difficult to define a Bessel function for the benefit of a non-mathematician–simply because such a complex idea cannot be defined except within a 'scaffolding' of mathematics.

It should be observed that the 'mathematical scaffolding,' and the 'philosophical scaffolding' are not different co-ordinate systems that are inapplicable to the world of our everyday experience. They are *extensions* of our everyday co-ordinate systems.

This brings an important recognition. The reason that 'mathematical truth' and 'philosophical truth' sometimes appear to contradict everyday common sense is because common sense is so short sighted. Common sense is in the position of the man in the boat surrounded by fog; the mathematician or the philosopher extend their scaffolding into the fog.

So mathematics, science and philosophy are running a parallel course with poetry and religion. This is the reason that James had to insist that his glimpse of 'ranges of distant fact' was *perceptual* and not conceptual. Science and philosophy also reach out towards those ranges of distant facts. *But they are inclined to take it for granted that the fog is a permanent human condition.*

This is an important realisation. There is a school of modern philosophy that denies that existentialism can ever have the precision required by a scientific philosophy. The above considerations show that, far from being 'unscientific,' existentialism is a logical extension of the idea of a scientific philosophy.

There is no *a priori* reason why mathematical truth should not be perceptual as well as conceptual. But there are certain difficulties in the way. Consider, for example, Arthur Koestler's description of a 'mystical experience' in his autobiography *The Invisible Writing*. Koestler was in a Spanish prison during the revolution; he was in danger of being shot. To pass away the time, he scratched mathematical formulae on the walls, including the formulae for an ellipse and a parabola, then went on to recall Euclid's proof that the number of primes is infinite.

'Since I had become acquainted with Euclid's proof at school, it had always filled me with a deep satisfaction that was aesthetic rather than intellectual. Now, as I recalled the method, and scratched the symbols on the wall, I felt the same enchantment.

'And then, for the first time, I suddenly understood the reason for this enchantment: the scribbled symbols on the wall represented one of the rare cases where a meaningful and comprehensive statement about the infinite is arrived at by precise and finite means. The infinite is a mystical mass shrouded in a haze; and yet it was possible to gain some knowledge of it without losing oneself in treacly ambiguities. The significance of this swept over me like a wave. The wave had originated in an articulate verbal insight; but this evaporated at once, leaving in its wake only a wordless essence, a fragrance of eternity, a quiver of the arrow in the blue. I must have stood there for some minutes, entranced with a wordless awareness that 'this is perfect – perfect'; until I noticed some slight mental discomfort nagging at the back of my mind – some trivial circumstance that marred the perfection of the moment. Then I remembered the nature of that irrelevant annoyance: I was, of course, in prison and might be shot. But this was immediately answered by a feeling whose verbal translation would be: 'So what? is that all? have you nothing more serious to worry about?' – an answer so spontaneous, fresh and amused as if the intruding annoyance had been the loss of a collar stud. Then I was floating on my back in a river of peace, under bridges of silence. It came from nowhere and flowed nowhere. Then there was no river and no I. The I had ceased to exist.' (Chapter 33.)

The first thing to note is that there is much here that echoes James's experience. 'And then, for the first time, I suddenly understand the reason for this enchantment.' The fog lifts, and he can see the boy skimming stones as well as the stones striking the water. The first step in this experience is that the mathematical formula ceases to be a mere formula; he suddenly *sees* its meaning and its connection with *reality*; conceptual knowledge has become perceptual.

But from this point on, we can see the difficulties. So far we can give precise meanings to Koestler's description. But when he speaks about an 'arrow in the blue,' about 'rivers of peace and bridges of silence,' we can only hope that we know what he is talking about. But it is possible to understand his indifference to the thought of death.

The 'self' that has been experiencing various fears and humiliations has been evoked by a narrow and trivial range of experience. The self that has, so to speak, become aware of Mozart and the stars, is contemptuous of this triviality. All the fear of imprisonment and death is included in this contempt. But even this new 'self,' responding with such delight to the horizons of distant fact, contains many elements that are associated with the trivial level. These are also shed, rejected; a god-like self, *with no element whatever in common with the old 'Arthur Koestler'* (except consciousness), now contemplates the mountain ranges of distant fact. Hence 'the I had ceased to exist.'

But now we begin to see the size of the problem. James's theory about mysticism and consciousness enables us to give a fairly precise meaning to Koestler's description. Even so, the understanding is strained. Now consider a further example of a similar experience. This is taken from a description by the French critic and poet, René Daumal, who died in 1944.

Daumal explains that, from a very early age, he has been interested in the problem of the 'beyond,' and that even at the age of six he has spent 'atrocious nights' terrified by the problem of death, of 'nothingness.' He attempted to keep his mind partly conscious during sleep, but found that 'my own organism gave me some serious warnings of the risks I was running.' He then (at the age of sixteen) decided to try anaesthetising himself with carbon tetrachloride, but, as far as possible, remaining conscious during the experiment. He describes how he succeeded in doing this. 'By this time, I was no longer capable of speech, even of interior speech; my mind travelled too rapidly to carry any words along with it.' The ordinary world, which he still perceived, had become strangely unreal, 'like having repeated a word over and over again until it shrivels and dies in your mouth.' The reason for this was that 'I had abruptly entered another world, *infinitely more real* . . . a concentrated flame of reality . . .' '. . . I feel the certainty of the existence of *something else*, a beyond, another world, or another form of knowledge.' He emphasises that, in this state of intense perception, he remained aware of the ordinary world and its relations; it was not blotted out, as in a dream. In the way that the physical world is realler than the world of concepts or ideas, so this 'other world' is realler than the physical world of everyday reality.

Daumal's account is some 4,000 words long, and he attempts to explain his 'insight' in some detail.[1] There would be no point in citing more of it here, since his attempts to explain the content of the insight are as vague as in most mystical experiences. But he speaks of the dangers of the experience, and compares them to that of Bluebeard's wife, who 'opens the door of the hidden room, and the horrible spectacle sears her innermost being as with a white hot iron.' He mentions that he escaped insanity only by good luck.

The main point to note about this description is that it agrees with James's theory of the 'man in the boat'; there is again the sense of *seeing further*, and of seeing this 'reality' of our everyday lives as a single, limited case among many others – rather as Einstein regards Euclidean geometry as one among an infinite number of geometrics.

What all this makes clear is that a 'new existentialism' must begin with the rather pedestrian task of pushing its scaffolding of language into these new realms. James foretold that we could not understand these changes in

1. Reprinted in *The Psychedelic Review,* No. 5, translated by Roger Shattuck.

consciousness in this generation or the next. But we shall never begin to understand them until we create the heavy machinery of language and concepts to map these new areas.

We encounter difficulties from the beginning. If we state that the 'new existentialism' is based upon a recognition that 'ordinary consciousness' tells us lies, and that there is 'something else, a beyond, another world' that should be the goal of philosophy, we are still speaking in the language of misunderstanding. There is no 'other world'; the 'ranges of distant fact' belong essentially to this world. If anything is an illusion, it is our present mode of consciousness; or rather, its content.

The desirable mental attitude can be explained by an analogy. One might be in the company of a confidence trickster, and *know* him to be a confidence trickster; yet be so impressed by his manner that one tends to disbelieve one's own knowledge, and to identify with the people who are taken in by him. Anyone who has been through an aesthetic experience similar to James's knows that his ordinary consciousness is limited, *and that therefore his sense of the value of existence is inaccurate*. This latter point is the important one, and the one upon which we must concentrate. It is the word 'values' that lands us at the heart of the problem of the method of the new existentialism. For our values are our most intimate response to our conscious perception of existence. What we regard as worth doing or not worth doing – that is our values.

There is a further interesting point which deserves to be mentioned in passing. Glimpses of horizons of distant fact may be rare in our lives; but almost every adult human being has had some 'mystical' experience, since almost every adult has experienced sexual excitement and sexual orgasm. If we examine sexual experience in the light of what has been said in the last chapters, we see that it is an excellent example of the 'man in the boat.' We are aware of a powerful compulsion that reaches beyond our present fears and inhibitions, but we cannot see its origin, which lies on the other side of the fog. The sexual orgasm itself is an apparently illogical sense of power and affirmation which, like Koestler's vision of infinity, transcends the present self and its fears and values. One writer on existentialism has described its basic theme as 'the fundamental alienation of beings from the source of power, meaning and purpose.' In the intensity of sexual experience, this alienation vanishes. Man is momentarily restored to the 'source of power, meaning and purpose.'

Hofmannsthal's Chandos Letter

But to return to the problem of language.

The school of linguistic philosophy – whose key figures are Wittgenstein and J. L. Austin – has recognised the inadequacy of 'everyday language,' which is like a machine in which all the parts are loose. Austin's 'philosophy' represents an attempt to 'tighten up' language to an unprecedented degree, with minute concentration upon the functions of words. The ordinary man approaches language as he approaches his car; it is something he knows how to *use* for his own purposes. The linguistic philosopher approaches language as a mechanic approaches a car; he wants to understand everything that happens under the bonnet.

This is obviously an important and necessary approach. But it is inclined to encourage a serious shortcoming in its practitioners: a tendency to lose sight of the real aims of philosphy. A car, after all, is an instrument for *getting somewhere*. Linguistic analysis is inclined to turn its practitioners into expert critics at the expense of their philosophical faculty which, like any other creative faculty, works largely upon insights and intuitions.

The linguistic philosophers are inclined to accuse existentialism of a systematic misuse of language; at best they are inclined to doubt whether the existentialist approach can lead, of itself, to the demand for linguistic precision which is a natural product of the critical approach. In fact, this is untrue. Existentialism is always preoccupied with a sense of the inadequacy of language.

The way in which this comes about can be seen if we consider the work of the Austrian poet Hugo von Hofmannsthal. Hofmannsthal gained a reputation in his teens with a number of lyric poems that have the same strange perfection of those of the young Rimbaud. By the time he was in his mid-twenties (at the end of the last century), this lyric gift had dried up. The reason, which becomes clear from the study of his letters, was an increasing sense of the inadequacy of language. The subtle, tortuous, oversensitive mind of Hofmannsthal began to feel that ordinary language is a mockery of what takes place underneath. This feeling is expressed in one of his most important prose works, *The Letter of Lord Chandos to Sir Francis Bacon*. Chandos writes to Bacon to explain his abandonment of literary activity. He writes:

'. . . I have completely lost the ability to think or speak of anything coherently. . . . At first . . . I experienced an inexplicable distaste for so much as uttering the words *spirit*, *soul* or *body*. . . . The abstract terms of which the tongue must avail itself as a matter of course in order to voice a judgement – these terms crumbled in my mouth like mouldy fungi.'

The sentiment of this passage would not be out of place in Ryle's *Concept of Mind*. But the sense of inner revelation here has also obvious links with William James's 'vastation' experience. Chandos goes on:

'Gradually, however, these attacks of anguish spread like a corroding rust. Even in familiar and humdrum conversation all the opinions which are generally expressed with ease and sleep-walking assurance became so doubtful that I had to cease altogether taking part in such talk. . . . As once, through a magnifying glass, I had seen a piece of skin on my little finger look like a field full of holes and furrows, So I now perceived human beings and their actions. I no longer succeeded in comprehending them with the simplifying eye of habit. For me, everything disintegrated into parts. . . .'

But the experience is not entirely negative – a mere rejection of what is normally called life. He has a sense of meaning which brings to mind Aldous Huxley's description of his mescalin experience:

'. . . filling . . . any casual object of my daily surroundings with an overflowing flood of higher life. . . . A pitcher, a harrow abandoned in a field, a dog in the sun, a neglected cemetery, a cripple, a peasant's hut – all these became the vessel of my revelation.'

The nature of his problem is made clear when he mentions that he is obsessed by the thought of the orator Crassus, who became so fond of a tame lamprey that he shed tears when it died. When someone reproached him for this, he replied: 'Thus have I done over the death of my fish as you have done over the death of neither your first nor second wife.' What is at issue here is the opposite of Heidegger's 'forgetfulness of Existence.' He has become so intensely aware of Existence that all language becomes a lie. The element of despair that enters into the Chandos letter is obviously due to the fact that language is the chief medium of communication between human beings – in some ways, the only medium. To reject communication is to retreat into a completely personal world, which is close to the world of madness. The only way out of this condition – which has so much in common with Sartre's 'nausea' – is to recognise that language must be developed until it is no longer inadequate.

The mention of Huxley makes clear the exact nature of the problem; it also makes it clear that it must be approached through psychology rather than through Austin's type of linguistic analysis. Let us ask the question: why does mescalin induce such totally different experiences in different people? To Huxley it brought a Hofmannsthal-type revelation. To R. H. Ward (who describes his experience in *A Drug Taker's Notes*) it brought certain semi-mystical insights, but also a horrifying vision of putrefaction and death. To the critic Raymond Mortimer, it brought only a sense of complete emotional dehydration, and a feeling of panic in case it had destroyed his emotions for ever.[1] To Sartre, it brought hallucinations of lobsters and 'nausea.'

The problem has nothing to do with the 'mystical' content of the experience. It is simply that we have so far no language to identify the subtle processes of such an experience.

It is for this reason that the development of the 'new existentialism' is so closely bound up with the development of ordinary clinical psychology. For most of the problems in understanding madness are problems of false assumptions, and therefore of language. (Typical of these is the assumption of James Mill that madmen could be reasoned out of their madness.) The distinction that ordinary

1. *Sunday Times*, 1955, reprinted in *Encore, the Sunday Times Book*, Second Year (1963).

language draws between sanity and madness may be useful in practice, but it has the same disadvantages as the pre-Newtonian hypothesis that the earth is the centre of the universe – that is to say, it quickly leads to absurd complications. Husserl's recognition of intentionality was equivalent to placing the sun in the centre of the solar system. But the meaning of Husserl's discovery for psychology was this: that the mind is not a machine whose ailments can be defined in terms of *external* pressures. Insanity is an act of surrender; as such, it is intentional. It is due to a breakdown in meaning-perception, in healthy response to environment, which in turn is due to a narrowing of the field of perception and of values; this narrowing is also, on a different level, intentional. But since most psychology is still tied up with mechanistic notions and the 'fallacy of passive perception,' it is hardly surprising if there has been no development of a language and conceptology to define these levels of intentionality. Sartre has further complicated the problem by constructing an ingenious psychology out of a mixture of Freudian determinism and phenomenology.[1]

This, then, must be grasped clearly: the 'new language' of existentialism will be created out of a patient attempt at phenomenological description of man's inner states, particularly the abnormal inner states that can be induced by drugs or by mental illness.

This means, of course, that the 'new existentialism' already exists, at least in embryo, in the work of many of the phenomenological and existential psychologists – Medard Boss, Ludwig Binswanger, Erwin Straus, Viktor Frankl, Igor Caruso, R. D. Laing, Abraham Maslow – as well as in the work of the transactional psychologists, and of a 'scientific philosopher' such as Michael Polanyi.

1. See last chapter.

A Note on Merleau-Ponty

I should also mention here that it can be found in a highly developed form in the work of the late Maurice Merleau-Ponty, particularly in *The Phenomenology of Perception*. Merleau-Ponty was concerned with a problem he inherited from Descartes – the problem of whether the mind is 'an automatic machine which needs an outside agent to set off its pre-established mechanisms,' or 'a pure, contemplative consciousness' imposed on 'a thing-like body.'[1] This led Merleau-Ponty to the study of the nervous system, and to the problem of 'the body as the giver of meaning.' His view is that the mind is neither a 'machine' nor a contemplative soul. It lies somewhere between the two. In order to establish its degree of freedom or of mechanism, Merleau-Ponty analyses the subtleties of the nervous system at considerable length (mostly in his book *The Structure of Behaviour*).[2]

Although Merleau-Ponty's approach is inclined, at times, to be over-mechanistic, he is too good a phenomenologist to fall into the kind of self-contradictions that one finds in Sartre's theories of the emotions and imagination.

The aim of Merleau-Ponty's philosophy is best described in his own words: 'to rediscover the structure of the perceived world through a process similar to that of an archaeologist. For the structure of the perceived world is buried under the sedimentations of later knowledge'.[3] This aim may sound modest enough in itself until we

1. See *The Primacy of Perception*, p. 4, Northwestern University.

2. Arthur Koestler's book *The Act of Creation* covers much of the same ground as *The Structure of Behaviour*, and, because of the directness of its approach, can be recommended to readers who find it difficult to get their bearings in Merleau-Ponty.

3. *The Primacy of Perception*, p. 5.

recollect that, for Husserl, perception is the basic mode of intentionality; to investigate the structure of the perceived world is to investigate our 'life-world' – that is to say, everything we do, everything we think, ultimately, everything we *are*. Here, Merleau-Ponty's philosophy connects up with that of Sartre. The whole point of such works as *The Flies* and *Huis Clos* is that man should not feel helpless in the face of an intractable world that was already there before he arrived. In making some highly conscious act of choice, he is only *extending* the basic activity of his consciousness in 'constituting' the perceived world.

To put this in extremely simple terms – and to risk oversimplifying it: man's trouble is that he possesses two kinds of freedom. One is 'subconscious'; it is the continual activity of 'constituting' the perceived and experienced world, of which we only become aware when it breaks down (as in 'nausea' or the 'vastation'). The other is the conscious freedom that enters into my act of deciding to protest about the H bomb or any other issue. The whole point is that I would certainly enter into far more acts of conscious freedom – that is to say, creative acts – if I were aware of *how far I am already committed to unconscious freedom*. Since one of the chief defects of human beings is their laziness and passivity, it follows that Merleau-Ponty is actually taking the most practical step towards bringing about an improvement in seeking to chart the geography of man's unconscious freedom.

A detailed appreciation – a critique – of Merleau-Ponty is beyond the scope of the present book. I only wish to point out that such works as *The Structure of Behaviour* and *The Phenomenology of Perception* – both of which derive directly from the later Husserl – may be taken as elementary textbooks of 'the new existentialism.'

CHAPTER FIVE

EVERYDAY CONSCIOUSNESS IS A LIAR

Let us be quite clear about the implications of all this, for they constitute a revolution in philosophy. 'Peak experiences' all seem to have the same 'content': that the chief mistake of human beings is to pay too much attention to everyday trivialities. We are strangely inefficient machines, utilising only a fraction of our powers, and the reason for this is our short sightedness. Koestler's 'mystical' insight made him feel that even the threat of death was a triviality that should be ignored; 'So what. . . . Have you nothing more serious to worry about?' Greene's whisky priest: 'It seemed to him, at that moment, that it would have been quite easy to be a saint.' Death reveals to us that our lives have been one long miscalculation, based on triviality. Proust's Marcel, when he tastes the cake dipped in tea, says 'the vicissitudes of life had become indifferent to me, its disasters innocuous. . . . I had ceased now to feel mediocre, accidental, mortal.' In his diary, Nijinsky, on the point of insanity, wrote: 'I am God, I am God.'

What is revolutionary about the new existentialism is this: it asks whether there is not some logical method of investigating such insights and weighing their content against our 'everyday consciousness.' Nijinsky's statement 'I am God' was not the rambling of a sick mind; it was an insight of the same type as those of Koestler, William

James and Proust; and we have agreed that these insights have a certain objective content. In that case, the question suggests itself: '*Was* he God?'

An empirical philosopher would reply: 'Clearly not. Next question. . . .' But this is an evasion – like Moore producing his watch to demonstrate that time is not an illusion. A more reasonable objection would be: 'Is there any logical method of investigating such a question?' To that we can answer: Yes – through the phenomenological examination of consciousness. This in turn implies the creation of a language and a set of concepts in terms of which we can discuss it.

I think we should now be able to see clearly the fundamental issue on which the 'new existentialism' differs from the older version. The old existentialism emphasises man's contingency. It says that since there is no God, there are no 'transcendental values' either. Man is alone in an empty universe; no act of his has any meaning outside itself – and its social context. Existentialism has removed the universal backcloth against which mediaeval man acted out his dreams, with a sense that everything he did would be brought up on judgement day. In its place, says Sartre, there is only the infinitude of space, which means that man's actions are of no importance to anyone but himself.

Phenomenology replies: We grant you, for the sake of argument, that all religious values are nonsense. But we cannot agree that man's everyday sense of his 'self-evident contingency' represents the truth either. Everyday consciousness is a liar, and most people have insights to this effect at least once a week. If they concentrated upon the matter, they would get such insights more frequently still. The question is simply how to give such insights a philosophical status, and how to investigate them.

Once we see this clearly, it becomes astonishing that anyone bothers to argue about it. Harley Granville Barker spoke of these insights as 'the secret life' (in a play of that title), and points out that *all* men, no matter how materialistic and trivial, draw their strength from 'the secret life.'

In other words, there *is* a standard of values 'external to human consciousness,' if we are talking about the everyday human consciousness that most of us make the foundation of our values. In fact, both Sartre and Heidegger recognise this in recognising that man gains a sense of 'authenticity' in the face of death.

Such a recognition is only a beginning. Inauthenticity is to feel futile, contingent, without purpose. Authenticity is to be driven by a deep sense of purpose. *Such a sense of purpose cannot exist unless we first make the assumption that our sense of contingency is a liar, and that there is a standard of values external to everyday human consciousness.*

In short, where both Sartre and Heidegger make a mistake is in supposing that the flash of authenticity experienced under the threat of death is a more or less 'mystical' sensation that cannot be carried over into ordinary human existence. It is not. It is a glimpse of a consciousness of purpose which, under certain circumstances, should be quite easily accessible to human beings. Once we have accepted James's idea that 'mystical consciousness' is only a change in the threshold of ordinary consciousness, the whole thing becomes more down-to-earth.

It might be mentioned, in passing, that this basic recognition differs in no fundamental respect from the metaphysics of the *Upanishads* or the *Bhagavad Gita*. The difference between the religious standpoint and the 'natural standpoint' is the difference between the 'external values system' of the new existentialism and the 'total contingency' of the old. (But I am speaking now of the metaphysics of religion, as distinguished from the element of dogma and the supernatural.)

This is the foundation. For biological reasons, we are 'blinkered,' like horses in the traffic. The blinkers are a device for enabling us to concentrate on the present and its problems. A painter who is painting a large canvas has to work with his nose to the canvas; but periodically he stands back to see the effect of the whole. These over-all glimpses renew his sense of purpose.

Man's evolution depends upon a renewal of the sense of over-all purpose. For several centuries now, the direction of our culture has been a concentration upon the minute, the particular. In the field of science, this has produced our present high level of technological achievement. In the field of culture, we have less reason for self-congratulation, for the concentration upon the particular – to the exclusion of wider meanings – has led us into a *cul de sac*. Yeats described the result as 'fish gasping on the strand' – a minute realism that has lost all drive and purpose.

I have said that the next step consists in a phenomenological analysis of consciousness. We have no language to describe these important inner-states.

In the remainder of this book, I shall attempt to make a beginning upon a systematic phenomenology of consciousness. It should be possible to at least lay down the broad outlines of such a 'new science.'

Let us begin with a consideration of the word 'values.' What is a value? It is a kind of 'rate of exchange.' If I say that a certain object is not worth what the shopkeeper is asking for it, I mean that I am not willing to exchange money for it. If I say that a certain task is 'not worth the effort,' I mean that I am not willing to exchange *vital energy* for the result it will obtain.

Everything that I experience causes a rise or fall in the immediate level of my vital energy. Eating when I am hungry, drinking when I am thirsty, causes a rise in the level of my vitality. A 'value' is that physical response of pleasure and vitality that I experience as I swallow food. So we might also say that *a value is a response*. This response determines what we consider 'worth doing.'

Religion and philosophy, of course, aim at absolute values. But we might also note that human beings in general aim at absolute values. Our life is an attempt to discard false values. A child enjoys cream cakes; but he discovers that too many of them make him sick; he therefore learns eventually not to over-indulge in cream cakes. The 'immediate' response to cream cakes is replaced by a more reasoned response that sees further.

But our value systems are not internally consistent; neither do they have to be. We adopt temporary systems of values according to the task in hand. A parent loves a child, but if the child needs correction, he places the love temporarily in abeyance and takes up the rod. He is actually practising what Husserl calls 'bracketing.' The same thing happens if I decide that I must finish a certain task in hand, even though there are other things I would prefer to do. I deliberately 'bracket out' my response (i.e. values) to the things I would prefer to do, and concentrate on the task that must be finished.

We are therefore capable of altering our immediate responses – and values – in favour of some more embracing value system. To some extent, therefore, every moment of our conscious lives depends upon the value systems we adopt.

Since the most ordinary act of living depends upon the handling of such complex 'values,' it is obviously important that our over-all, basic values should be very clear indeed, to prevent confusion. But here we immediately encounter the great problem. A value is a response, an immediate warm flow of vitality and optimism. But since our consciousness is so limited, it is precisely our 'ultimate' values that are *not* responses. A saint like Ramakrishna may be able to establish immediate vital contact with his deepest values; but most of us have to work on in the dark.

All this talk about values makes the problem sound somewhat abstract, when it is anything but. It is purely practical. Our lives are enveloped in moods, in the ebb and flow of energy. The human beings we refer to as 'great' have seized the sense of purpose that comes with the moods of optimism, and tried to live by it. The problem is an absurd one. It is like the sequence in the Charlie Chaplin film where the tramp meets a man who is kind and generous to him when drunk, and rude and violent when sober. Which is the 'real' man? Or is the question unanswerable, as Pirandello seems to imply in various plays that deal with the same kind of subject? The question may sound 'meaningless' to an empiricist philosopher, but it is of vital importance to every human being who is more than half alive. Human beings experience life as a series of moods. (These 'moods' are actually intentional value-judgements.) Each 'mood' seems to offer them a different piece of advice on the question of how to live. In ages of faith, man possessed religious belief to act as a compass to steer him through his moods, but in an age of humanism, he is at the mercy of the 'moods.' Each mood seems to reveal the 'reality' of the world; in moods of extreme pessimism, life is a cheat, a swindler, and man's optimism is sheer gullibility; in moods of optimism, the pessimism seems to have been the outcome of feebleness and poor-spiritedness. Our usual state of mind is somewhere between the two; we plod on passively, avoiding great risks, hoping for the best. Obviously, we require an *objective* standard, so that we are no longer ships that change our course with every wind.

In saying this, I have stated the central aim of the 'new existentialism.' We immediately become aware of the complexity of the problem. A relativist would dismiss it by saying: How can you decide that the world is one thing or the other? But this is premature defeatism. One might say, in the case of Charlie Chaplin's drunk, that it is meaningless to ask which is his 'true' character: that drink simply reveals another aspect of his character. But any competent psychologist would set out to analyse the man's character in terms of basic impulses and their frustration, and would emerge eventually with an answer that would be somewhere near to the 'objective truth.' At least, it would be nearer than the defeatist idea that there's no such thing.

So when attempting to assess the degree of objective justification for the optimistic and pessimistic attitudes to human existence, we have to be prepared for a fairly complicated task. But once we pose the question of what constitutes human values, the problem ceases to look so formidable. We have taken a step as decisive as the realisation that the sun is the fixed point in our planetary system. The shifting sands cease to shift. An apparently insoluble task suddenly begins to yield to our effort.

The new existentialism consists of a phenomenological ex-

amination of consciousness, with the emphasis upon the problem of what constitutes human values. And since moods of optimism and insight are less accessible than moods of depression and life-devaluation, the phenomenology of life-devaluation constitutes the most valuable field of study.

The Analysis of Language

Before I consider this problem in more detail, I must enlarge a point made in the previous chapter.

The analysis of consciousness is only half the task. The other half consists in the analysis of language. In this field, Wittgenstein was the great forerunner.

It was Wittgenstein who pointed out that we tend to treat language as a unity as if the language of Shakespeare, Hegel, Beatrix Potter and Freud all belonged somewhere on the same scale. Wittgenstein recognised that this apparent unity is actually a conglomerate of a number of different language systems (or 'games,' as he preferred to call them), each with different sets of 'rules.' Different 'games' may have as little in common as football has with poker or cowboys and Indians. He used the simile of the cabin of a locomotive, full of different types of lever; some have to be pulled, others pushed, others wound in a circle, others worked back and forth . . . and so on. Words have just as many functions. Only in the simplest and most primitive language games does a word correspond simply to an object.

Wittgenstein's intention was apparently negative; he wished to show that most philosophy is a misunderstanding of language. But the deeper aim has much in common with Husserl's; he aimed at doing *foundation work* on which it would be possible to build a philosophy. In fact, his aim is obviously complementary to Husserl's; one was interested in a phenomenology of perception, the other of language.

It may be that, in terms of priorities, the phenomenology of language is more important than the phenomenology of perceptions and values. This would certainly be so if the 'new existentialism' aimed at being only a description of the 'human condition' in a general sense – for the scientist must begin by making sure that his measuring instruments are accurate. But since the 'new existentialism' concentrates upon a phenomenological account of perceptive-consciousness and value-consciousness, it has inbuilt safeguards in its active and permanent preoccupation with language.

Nevertheless, the point should be made here that a phenomenology of language is as vital to the development of a new existentialism as the phenomenology of values. The new existentialism is not all psychology.

Not the least important feature of the 'new existentialism' is that it is able to unite the two major traditions of twentieth century philosophy: linguistic empiricism and phenomenological existentialism.

CHAPTER SIX

THE POWER OF THE SPECTRE

Existentialism said: There are no transcendental values; therefore man should not look for values outside his everyday consciousness. The new existentialism replies: You have overlooked the third possibility. There are states of consciousness that are not 'everyday consciousness' and which are not 'transcendental' either. These produce a definite sense of values and purpose. If we investigate these properly, man may be able to replace his old dogmatic religious values with a scientifically objective set of external values.

This summarises the purpose of the 'new existentialism,' and provides it with a direction in which to advance, and with a philosophical method.

The first thing that strikes us about the 'new existentialism' is that it is more immediate and personal than the existentialism of Sartre and Heidegger. It deals with the most immediate problem we can experience, with our actual living response to everyday existence: a territory that has so far been regarded as the concern of the novelist or poet. But it does not differ in any fundamental respect from the existentialism of Kierkegaard, Sartre and Heidegger. It only attempts to go further.

Let us be frank about this. One of the reasons that the 'old existentialism' found itself immobilised was that it tried so hard to compromise with academic philosophy. To a large extent, the difficulties encountered in a text of Jaspers, Heidegger or Sartre are the difficulties that the author feels to be necessary to an academically respectable philosophy.

The truth is that existentialism has more in common with science fiction than with academic philosophy. Its concern is 'the fundamental alienation of beings from the source of power, meaning and purpose'.[1] This clearly implies that the central effort of human life is directed at an alignment with this 'source of power and purpose.' We must repeat that this need not be interpreted in a religious sense. Human consciousness is narrow; James's glimpse of 'ranges of distant fact' produced precisely that sense of power, meaning and purpose that we are speaking of. Human boredom, the human sense of contingency and lack of purpose, are due largely to our 'blinkered' consciousness; and our blinkered consciousness is, as we have seen, an 'intentional' safety device.

To express this problem in science-fiction terms: it would seem that there is some mysterious agency that wishes to hold men back, to prevent them from gaining full use of their powers. It is as if man contained an invisible parasite, whose job is to keep man unaware of his freedom. Blake called this parasite 'the spectre.' In certain moments of vitality and inspiration, the spectre releases his hold, and man is suddenly dazzlingly aware of what he *could* do with his life, his freedom. He has every reason to be delighted. He has evolved slowly over a million or so years, and his evolution has been a slow acquisition of power over nature. In recent centuries his advance has been phenomenal. Science has opened up new mental worlds, showed him how to use his intelligence for the

1. William Kimmel: *The Search for Being*, Introduction.

acquisition of knowledge and power, as well as affording him the leisure and material prosperity to explore his new powers. But at this very moment in history, the spectre seems to be making a new effort to defeat us. With all our leisure, our knowledge, the prospect of endless new realms to conquer, we have never been so bored and depressed, and the increased rate of suicide and neurosis is becoming one of our major social problems.

On the other hand, if man can become fully conscious of the enemy and turn the full battery of his attention on it, the problem is solved. Man will solve the problem of 'alienation from the source of power, meaning and purpose', and a new phase of evolution will have begun, the phase of the truly human – or superhuman, as Nietzsche called it.

We might justify this 'science-fiction' account of the problem by pointing out that Plato was the first to employ it; in the *Symposium*, Aristophanes explains that the gods decided to prevent human beings from becoming supermen by dividing them into male and female, so that they would lose sight of ultimate objectives in sexual romanticism. This is not far from the phenomenological account – except that, for the phenomenologist, the division is between passive consciousness and an intentional subconscious mind.

But whether we accept the myths or not, we must recognise that the power behind human evolution has been man's intuition of *freedom*, and his identification of freedom with knowledge. Modern pessimism – whether it is philosophical or of the fashionable literary variety – only exists *by ignoring its inherent self-contradictions*. If we instinctively acknowledge human greatness as a value – that is, if we agree that a Jesus is in some way preferable to Judas Iscariot, that Beethoven is a more valuable human being than Al Capone – then we are subscribing to the basic human vision of freedom. To hold these values and to declare that life is meaningless is self-contradictory.

It is extremely important to grasp the notion that *man does not yet exist.* This is not intended as a paradox or a play on words; it is literally true. The animal's freedom is only a freedom to respond to external stimuli. In his book *The Living Brain*, Grey Walter says: 'The brain of lion, tiger, rhinoceros and other powerful animals also lacks the mechanism of imagination, or we should not be here to discuss the matter. . . . The nearest creature to us, the chimpanzee, cannot retain an image long enough to reflect on it.' So the life of an animal is largely a matter of conditioned reflexes. This means that most animals live simply in a perpetual present; they are little more than machines with consciousness.

This is also true of man; he also lives in a perpetual present; the mood of yesterday contradicts the mood of today. But while the animal is carried along passively on the stream of time, man has certain capacities that enable him to resist the current or to look into the future. The animal is carried along *by* time like a leaf in the stream; man is, in a real sense, a 'time traveller'; he has a small motor that can enable him to navigate the stream. His invention of language was the first step towards this 'conquest of time.' Language 'fixes' experiences, and places the experience of the past on equal footing with the experience of the present.

The development of imagination was bound to follow the development of language, since it is only one step from 'labelling' a past experience to conjuring up its mental image.

The next step was the development of thought *for its own*

sake. The first man to while away his leisure in working out some simple problem in mathematics had taken one of the greatest steps forward in the history of the race. Most activities we do 'for their own sake' – gardening, playing games, hunting – lead nowhere in particular. Thinking for its own sake has created civilisation and all the arts and sciences.

The use of imagination and intellect brought man his greatest vision: of the idea of a life lived at a level of intensity and purpose that is impossible for the mere animal. This is where man became, for the first time, painfully aware of his limitations. The wings of imagination are powerful, but they cannot support the mind for long periods. Science has developed so quickly because the scientific imagination has been aided by the discipline of the scientific *method*. The artist has had no comparable discipline or method. Neither, until recently, has the philosopher. The scientists of the nineteenth century worked together; when one made a discovery, it contributed to the general pool of scientific knowledge. By comparison, the artists, poets and philosophers were all working alone, each in his ivory tower, and each one had to learn by his own mistakes. It is very rare for the vision of one major artist or philosopher to be carried over to another artist or philosopher, who in turn carries it further.

It is this capacity for imagination that gives man his uniqueness, his potential of superhumanity. But how can man learn to use this imagination to conquer the 'fallacy of passive consciousness,' to reach out to the 'ranges of distant fact'?

The first task is to break ourselves of certain old habits of thought. Of these, the 'passive fallacy' is by far the most difficult; it will only disappear as a result of a total change of viewpoint. But other aspects of the problem are easier to attack. For example, it is possible for us to develop a genuine insight into the meanings of the words 'imagination' and 'freedom.'

Let us consider an example that Sartre offers in *The Transcendence of the Ego* of the paradoxical nature of freedom. He cites the case of a young married woman who feels a compulsion to go to the window and summon men like a prostitute. Nothing in her upbringing could account for this. Her urge to betray her husband horrifies her, and she recognises it as neurotic. Sartre says that she is suffering from a 'vertigo of freedom.' We can see immediately that she is experiencing the same compulsion that Dostoevsky examines in so many of his novels. (Most of Stavrogin's actions in *Devils* are impelled by the same urge; so is that scene in *The Idiot* where a number of people at a party decide to describe their meanest action.) Poe wrote a story called *The Imp of the Perverse* about this curious urge to do something that is contrary to one's wellbeing.

The 'vertigo of freedom' explanation throws no real light on the problem; it only appears to do so because we associate the words with our fear of heights. For Sartre, freedom is essentially negative, an emptiness into which one is tempted to fling oneself.

The notion of the 'indifference threshold', however, gives us a deeper insight into the question. Man is a purposive animal, but he is trapped in the present, which denies him a sense of purpose. Stavrogin (in *Devils*) specifically states that his problem is that he has enormous strength *but no purpose to which to apply it.* Therefore his perverse actions are a protest against this narrow present that traps him and denies him outlet for his strength.

Man is instinctively aware that he is a 'purposive' animal, that he was not intended to live passively in the present. He therefore feels an instinctive protest against the present and its values. If he is not far-sighted enough to see to new horizons of purpose, he may still feel a deep dissatisfaction with his present values. Sartre mentions that nothing in the young girl's past or training could explain her urge to summon men. But it is precisely because there is nothing in her upbringing to explain it that she feels the urge. Her upbringing is 'respectable'; it tells her that 'nice' girls do not give themselves to strange men, that they become good bourgeois wives and mothers. Her sense of her own possibilities revolts against this static vision of her future; one might say that it is her higher-self, her super-conscious mind, that grins sardonically and urges her timid, bourgeois self to self-destruction.

This becomes even clearer in a story by Goethe called *The Honest Attorney*, which has much in common with Sartre's anecdote. A young wife is left alone by her husband, who sets out on a long voyage. He tells her that she may take a lover, provided the lover is discreet. The idea genuinely horrifies her; she has every intention of remaining faithful. But after some weeks of loneliness and boredom, she finds that her mind compulsively returns to the very idea that horrifies her. Eventually, she makes advances to a well-conducted young attorney. He tells her that he would be delighted to become her lover, except that he made a vow to live like a hermit for a year. The vow still has some months to run. However, if she would be willing to share it with him, fasting and sleeping on the floor, they can become lovers in half the time. . . . The girl agrees. Her fasting has the effect that the 'lover' expected; it stiffens her moral fibre, destroys her boredom, and renews her determination to be faithful to her husband.

Here we see the destructive effect of boredom, as in

Sartre's anecdote; but Goethe sees deeper than Sartre, recognising that the girl's 'perverseness' is due to a frustrated need for a purpose. The moral of his story is not that freedom overflows the mind, but that man is a purposive animal.

Poe's *Imp of the Perverse* serves as an even better example. The central character is a murderer, a man who has killed an old man for his money. It is a perfect murder and he feels no fear of detection. For a long time he delights in his safety. Then one day, he reflects that he is safe so long as he is not fool enough to confess. Immediately, he has the feeling of the wife in Goethe's story – the desire to do something that horrifies him. Ultimately, he can resist it no longer, and confesses.

The story is a significant variation on the Dostoevskian theme because the hero is a criminal. Most human beings are governed by expediency, but the criminal is the man whom expediency has blinded to his evolutionary purpose.

I have dealt with this question of the philosophical significance of crime elsewhere,[1] but it deserves to be restated here. The key lies in Shaw's remark that we judge the artist by his highest movements, the criminal by his lowest. In a sense, our response to a poem or a piece of music involves a more positive sense of goodness than any of our moral judgements. If I help a blind man across the road, my action may be only dimly connected with my sense of moral values; I may feel thoroughly bored by it, and do it solely out of a sense of duty. There is no possibility of such emotional 'double exposure' in my response to a poem or a symphony. If I am in any way detached from it – perhaps because I know it too well – then my response will lack intensity, or vanish altogether.

1. In the preface to *An Encyclopedia of Murder.*

Now it is possible to take a thoroughly 'positivist' view about good and evil: to declare that they are mere conventions of social behaviour. Or we may take the view that *Waiting for Godot* is an accurate account of the human situation, and that life is meaningless: in that case, the terms good and evil also become meaningless, in any transcendental sense. But to read an account of a murder case instantly evokes a reaction that is naked and unreflective as our response to a symphony: a sense of waste, of stupidity, of false values. We become aware that, even if we think life meaningless, the life of a murderer seems *more meaningless* than our own – an obvious impossibility unless we possess a powerful subconscious sense of values.

In his autobiography *Doubtful Schoolmaster*, Hugh Heckstall Smith tells an anecdote that is relevant here. One of his colleagues was a positivist and a follower of Comte. One day as they entered the staff room, the positivist remarked of another master: 'I can't bear that man – I get the feeling that he's evil.' Heckstall Smith enquired: 'You mean he doesn't conduce to the greatest good of the greatest number?' The positivist looked baffled, and had to admit that he didn't mean anything of the sort; he meant something far more immediate and intuitive than a social theory of good and evil.

Our response to a murder – and to crime in general – proves that we possess a sense of values that lies deeper than everyday consciousness – a feeling that life is not here to be wasted. Once the existence of this sense of values is recognised, the 'perverseness' noted by Dostoevsky and Poe ceases to be a problem. In committing a murder, Poe's hero had destroyed his freedom; he now thinks of himself primarily as 'a murderer,' a fixed identity. He looks continually backwards to this act that settled his identity so irrevocably. He ceases to be a man with a future and becomes a man with a past. To confess is to restore his freedom.[1]

In short, man's 'perverseness,' far from being a proof of the basic meaninglessness of human existence, reveals his essential nature as a 'purposive animal.' It shows his two levels in conflict: the everyday self, with its desire for security and material rewards, and the evolutionary self that is inclined to regard the other with contempt.

Mencius says: 'Those who follow the part of themselves that is great become great men; those who follow the part of themselves that is little become little men.' This division of man into two 'selves' may seem an oversimplification, but it has the advantage of explaining the major paradoxes of human freedom. Sartre's view of the ego as a principle that unifies man's various actions and impulses completely fails to explain how this ego can come into conflict with itself. It fails, for example, to explain the 'perverseness' of a man like T. E. Lawrence, with his strong tendency to self-laceration, which is easily explained on the Blakeian assumption of conflicting selves – the evolutionary self and the 'spectre.' (The 'spectre,' of course, is the limited everyday self, with its tendency to laziness and materialism.) In fact, the whole 'outsider' phenomenon (which I analysed in the book of that title) reveals the conflict between man's two levels.

I have already stated (in Part One) that it is possible to base a new form of psychology on these recognitions: that

1. It might be objected that many people are interested in murder because they feel a curious and ambiguous form of admiration for the murderer. This is true, but it is a question of inauthentic imagination; the murderer is vaguely identified with the rebel, the adventurer. Synge, in the *Playboy of the Western World*, shows what happens when such inauthentic imagination is confronted with the 'real thing'; it recoils with horror, recognising that murder is the outcome of brutality and stupidity, not of creative rebellion.

man is by nature a purposive creature, who develops neuroses when purpose is denied him. This is a matter that deserves further comment, since the 'new existentialism' is so deeply concerned with psychology.

Predictably, phenomenology emphasises the 'intentional' element in mental illness. In an early work, *Sketch of a Theory of the Emotions*, Sartre propounded a view of the emotions as an attempt to 'work magic.' Normally, I can more or less handle the problems of my experience. But if an insoluble problem presents itself – a problem that makes me feel totally helpless – I reverse the process and 'transform' my own consciousness. For example, if someone points a gun at me, I may faint, in the way that an ostrich buries its head in the sand. The fainting is illogical, of course. It is a kind of wishful thinking that if I faint, the gunman will go away. This is why Sartre calls such a reaction 'magic'; for magic is also wishful thinking. It is not, of course, *reflective* wishful thinking, but a spontaneous reaction.

It is only one step from this to the phenomenological view of mental illness as a self-protective gesture. This view has been explored by 'existential psychologists' like Ludwig Binswanger, Medard Boss and R. D. Laing. It helps to explain, for example, the mental breakdown of a man like Schumann, who feels increasingly that his music is threatened by physical and economic problems, until he feels he is no longer able to cope with his experience, and retreats into melancholia. On the other hand the case of Strindberg is an example of successful 'magic.' His problems – largely his own fault – lead him to build up an elaborate persecution neurosis, in which he believes he is constantly pursued by invisible enemies. He actually writes a number of autobiographical books while in this state of insanity, and then – after a mystical conversion –

emerges more or less sane, to write the remarkable plays of his last period. Unlike Schumann (who was always terrified of insanity) he does not waste his vitality in self-criticism and fear, and so never becomes his own enemy as thoroughly as Schumann did.

The views I have outlined above form the basis of existential psychiatry as practised by Binswanger and Boss (although it should be mentioned that it is based upon the analyses of Heidegger rather than Sartre). The 'new existentialism' is essentially a deepening of these foundations.

It is difficult for the sane person to understand the mental universe of the insane. (John Stuart Mill's father thought it should be possible to 'reason' maniacs out of their madness.) This inability is mainly due to the false assumptions of the same. What we find puzzling is how anyone could react in an 'insane' way to our sane and orderly universe. This is simply one of the forms of the 'fallacy of passive perception.' The universe appears orderly because we unconsciously limit our perceptions – the same limitation that is, at the present, the chief barrier to human evolution. Mescalin removes this 'filter' from the perceptions, and overwhelms us with the material that we normally exclude.

It might seem, then, that what we are suggesting is that the madman's reaction to the universe is the 'sane' one; but this would be untrue. If we removed the blinkers from the eyes of a horse, it might well have a nervous breakdown in the traffic of a modern city. The horse's driver does not need blinkers because he has more self-control, a wider understanding of what is going on: in short, more intelligence and self-discipline. In fact, the horse's nervousness in traffic is due mostly to incomprehension, to instinctive – and quite groundless – fears.

In short, we must distinguish 'true sanity' from the sanity of short-sightedness and limitation. True sanity is the 'driver's' sanity – to see the chaos and to be above it. The present need – in psychology – is for a scientific investigation of these areas beyond normal consciousness: to explore them by means of drugs, and to 'map' them by means of phenomenological analysis.

In his story *The Wall*, Sartre has a passage that illustrates his theory of the emotions, and that enables us to go a step further into the phenomenology of value-consciousness. The character in *The Wall* is sentenced to death in a Spanish prison. Since he is completely helpless, he allows his pessimistic vision to become universal. Like Ecclesiastes, he devalues everything. It is the fable of the fox and the grapes, with life as the sour grapes.

This passage is of interest for two reasons. To begin with, it never seems to have struck Sartre to ask whether his own pessimistic vision, as developed in *Being and Nothingness*, is not a personal 'magic' response to a world in which he feels helpless. (It is significant that Sartre's optimistic philosophy of commitment and social change dates from the days of his rise to fame, immediately after the war.) The second point is that the situation in *The Wall* can be taken as a symbol of the general life situation.

Sartre's hero, Pablo Ibbieta, is condemned to death. All alleyways of escape are closed. Yet this is not quite true. For he *does* escape – by accidentally betraying a comrade. One might say therefore that he had *some* ground for hope all the time. But hope would have cost too much vital energy; his general 'life devaluation' was easier. It was also possible for him to make some enormous effort to escape – to work out a plan to disarm a guard, to bribe an official, to file away the bars of the cell . . . and so on. But he does not want to live *enough*. He has assessed the situation and decided to make no effort.

His situation is limited by the prison walls, and by the death waiting outside in the yard. In most everyday situations, the limiting factors are not so obvious; but they are there. We decide what is worth doing by taking a kind of general survey of the universe and our own individual lives. Naturally, the main element in this assessment is the physical reality actually present. This surrounds us like a prison; it *is* a prison, since we can never escape our limited field of vision. (This is obviously the reason that we love wide views and natural grandeur; the prison walls retreat.) There are also various threats and problems to be solved: none as absolute as death; but then, death itself is not an absolute threat, since it can always be evaded on specific occasions. Since, then, we are all in Pablo Ibbieta's situation all the time – or most of it – we respond more or less as he does: by 'devaluing' the world to a greater or lesser extent. If we could once *grasp* this with genuine insight, we would instantly become aware of the extent to which consciousness is intentional; it would be the first and most important step in the direction of a creative phenomenological attitude to our own existence.

This kind of application of existential psychology is not merely a sub-department of the 'new existentialism'; it is a vital part of its substance. For the 'new existentialism' is a revolution in psychology. It is the recognition that the usual distinction between sanity and insanity is a false one. *We are all insane*; the difference between Napoleon and a madman who believes he is Napoleon is a difference in degree, not in kind; both are acting on a limited set of assumptions.

Once we recognise this, we also recognise that the 'new

existentialism' is an effort to be truly 'sane.' At present, the gap between the sane man and the maniac is very small indeed. As William James rightly understood, the 'hour' can strike for any of us. Remove a few of the walls of illusion, and the sane man becomes insane. Once this is understood, we have placed psychology on a new and sounder foundation.

But a closer look at Sartre's theory of the emotions will serve as a final illustration of the difference in approach between the 'old' and the 'new existentialism.' It happens to go to the very root of the difference between them.

Sartre's account of negative emotions as a projection seems, on the face of it, accurate enough. He is only stating what we already know, that emotional responses are intentional. When the world gets 'out of control,' Sartre says, we try to avoid facing this fact by projecting emotion on it – rather as a person who has trodden on a rake immediately looks around for someone to blame. If I see something horrible – let us say, a gruesome accident in the street – my whole 'world' becomes horrible. This may seem to be no advantage: but at least, it makes the world seem 'all of a piece,' so that the accident now ceases to be something irrational and exceptional that challenges my vitality; it is now grimly logical. I can adjust my conduct to this new grim logic for a while, and allow time to wear away the impression; in this way I once more gain control of my world.

This is Sartre's account. We may feel there are some weak points in it, but let us accept it for the moment. The question now arises: But what about positive emotions, like joy? Surely they are not an attempt at self-deception (which is what 'magic' amounts to)? But Sartre's theory depends upon convincing us that they are.

He claims that the world is always complex and difficult, a perpetual challenge; therefore, if we feel joy, it is a deliberate attempt to blind ourselves to the reality. A man who feels joy at seeing his mistress, for example, is hiding from himself all the negative complexities of their relation, his underlying awareness that we are all basically alone and basically selfish, and allowing himself to be deceived into a sense of security and happiness. In other words, says Sartre, since the world can never justify the emotion of joy, it follows that all joy must be self-deception.

It is not difficult to understand how Sartre arrives at such an account of the emotions. Graham Greene has described how, in his teens, he experienced a kind of emotional exhaustion that made the whole world seem pointless; if someone pointed out a beautiful scene, he would recognise that it was beautiful, but fail to *feel* it.

Once one has had this experience of the world as something meaningless and pointless, it is only one step to feeling that our emotions are an attempt to transform this indifference – rather as the doting mother of a completely heartless son will manage to read love and affection into his indifference.

This argument has devastating results if carried into the field of poetry and beauty in general. Aldous Huxley had already made a similar point in an essay on *Wordsworth in the Tropics*, asserting that Wordsworth read his pantheism *into* nature, and that he would have found it more difficult if confronted by the savagery of nature in the tropics. If the romantic poet's love of beauty is dismissed as a projection of his wishes on to an indifferent nature, then the very foundation stone of existentialism is destroyed – for I have pointed out that existentialism is no more than a developed form of romanticism.

Let us consider the field of sex, for Freud also invokes the concept of magic in using the word 'fetish' in this context. At first, this only seems to support Sartre's arguments. A lover steals a handkerchief from the girl he adores. He knows that it is merely a piece of cotton, but he projects his emotions on to it and carries it next to his heart. He is using the handkerchief as a magical substitute for the girl. This immediately raises the question of how far his attitude to the girl is also a projection of purely personal emotions – how far it is a case of Don Quixote and Dulcinea. If he marries her, he will certainly cease to feel this magic intensity; is this not another way of saying that it is self-delusion?

But let us approach the matter from another angle, and apply a little phenomenology. Consider, first of all, the poetic or creative emotion. Let us take the case of a scientist or mathematician stumbling upon a discovery that opens a whole new field of investigation, We can say that his joy is an attempt to conceal from himself that his ignorance is still immense, but this is an upside down way of looking at it. His joy is the joy we feel as obstacles collapse, *as the field of our freedom abruptly increases*.

One thing to note about his joy is that it reduces his surroundings to negation. If he notices them at all, it will be to project his joy, admittedly. But most probably, he does not notice his surroundings; his mind is concentrated upon his inner vision of freedom. Insofar as he notices his surroundings, he *tends to see them freshly*. His mind does not settle upon them heavily, as it does when he is bored or depressed; it lights on them swiftly, like a butterfly, and is off again.

The same quality distinguishes the poetic experience. The mind hovers *above* objects, and sees them freshly, as on the first day of a holiday. When we read Wordsworth's sonnet on Westminster Bridge, it does not surprise us to learn that he was setting out on a journey when he wrote it.

In other words, the poetic experience is the experience of mental freshness, of mental power and freedom, that we also encounter in the case of scientific discovery. The early novels of H. G. Wells are suffused with an exhilaration which is at once a sense of poetry and of scientific enthusiasm. The essence of this experience is the mind's feeling of hovering like a bird, of not being dragged down by the gravitational pull of the 'ordinary.'

Now let us consider this gravitational pull of the ordinary. If I am brought up in surroundings that I associate with misery and pain, I shall feel it difficult to experience poetic emotions in these suroundings. If I happen to be in such surroundings when I receive a letter saying that I have been left a fortune, my joy will tend to be damped by the surroundings – although it will, of course, also confer new associations on the surroundings.

Now consider the phenomenon of boredom. Let us suppose I take a job in an office that strikes me as particularly dreary. For the first few days, I manage to keep my mind alive by a considerable mental effort – and perhaps by keeping a volume of poetry hidden in my desk drawer. But after a few days, the struggle becomes impossible because the surroundings are now associated with boredom. There is another factor that increases and intensifies this boredom: my 'forgetfulness of existence' of my surroundings. For the first few days, they are at least strange to me. After that, they become 'symbols'; I notice them only dimly. This means that I am more than ever at the mercy of my mental image of them, which is imbued with boredom. My 'automatic pilot' has taken over my perceptions. The usual role of this 'automatic pilot' is to free my mind for more important tasks; but since I am condemned to the trivial, his only effect is to hand me over to my defeat. If this canker of boredom is allowed to eat deeply enough into me, it will rob me of all my energy, all my creative delight, so that even a beautiful scene will fail to arouse any response.

Now we see that Sartre's position depends upon his assertion that to see the world as meaningless and indifferent is to see it 'truthfully,' with distortion or projection. It is, in fact, a basic and primal perception, before 'magic' has had a chance to transform it. But the above phenomenological analysis shows that, on the contrary, boredom and meaninglessness are a fairly complicated *end-product*, not a primal perception at all. Like misery and pain, boredom is a projection on to my surroundings. It is true that my surroundings are neutral. But if I experience beauty, I am not *projecting* beauty on to my surroundings. I am simply experiencing my *real inner freedom*, which the complex nature of my response to existence usually conceals from me.

Sartre's mistake – which Aldous Huxley repeats in his Wordsworth essay – is in reversing the processes in the perception of beauty. Admittedly, the poet abets the confusion by declaring that a hill or lake *is* beautiful, as if the beauty were inherent. But Coleridge, in his ode *Dejection* (which describes a state of emotional exhaustion like that of Sartre or Greene) states unambiguously:

> 'I may not hope from outward forms to win
> The passion and the life, *whose fountains are within*' (my italics).

That is to say, it is not true that a hill or a lake 'is' beautiful. The poet sees it as a symbol of an inner freedom which he experiences directly. If he chooses to make hills or lakes symbols of this freedom, it is in the hope that the symbol can later be used to re-invoke the freedom itself.

The same argument, of course, applies to the sexual question. It is true that the lover 'projects' emotion into the handkerchief – and into the girl herself. But he does so because the girl symbolises for him a certain freedom, a certain fulfilment, a certain richness and intensity of existence. The experience of 'being in love' also has the effect described by William James – of widening the horizon of facts that are present to consciousness. If we agree with James that this is an authentic 'mystical' experience, and not a delusion, then the Sartrian criticism of love is seen to miss the point.

The basic fallacy in Sartre's theory of the emotions is the one I have already pointed out in connection with *Nausea*: the notion that this vision of a reality that is at the same time meaningless and 'horrible' is a fundamental perception of truth: that it is somehow non-intentional. This is simply bad phenomenology, and contradicts Sartre's assertion that all perception is perception *of* something – i.e. that unless the perception were intentional, you would see nothing at all. The fact is that the perception that Sartre calls 'nausea' is intentionalised by negative emotions, like fear or defeat. This does not make it any 'deeper' than a perception intentionalised by joy.

The only answer to this argument is to declare that man's inner freedom – the source of joy – is a delusion, and that we are actually machines. But Sartre does not take this stand; he insists on the reality of that inner freedom that is the basis of the creative experience.

All this should make it clear that Sartre's thought is a mass of inner contradictions. But I should make it clear that the aim of this demonstration is not primarily to discredit Sartre, who is one of the most important and stimulating thinkers of our time. It is to demonstrate the *inevitability* of the 'new existentialism' by showing that the 'old pessimistic existentialism' disintegrates of its own accord when examined closely.

The 'new existentialism' accepts man's experience of his inner freedom as basic and irreducible. Our lives consist of a clash between two visions: our vision of this inner freedom, and our vision of contingency; our intuition of freedom and power, and our everyday feeling of limitation and boredom. The problem cannot be reduced to simpler terms. The 'new existentialism' concentrates the full battery of phenomenological analysis upon the everyday sense of contingency, upon the problem of 'life-devaluation.' This analysis helps to reveal how the spirit of freedom is trapped and destroyed; it uncovers the complexities and safety devices in which freedom dissipates itself. It suggests mental disciplines through which this waste of freedom can be averted.

For practical purposes, man may be regarded as a dual being, continually at war with himself. One of his selves is cautious, limited, materialistic, confined to the present. He is a born slave and coward; his creed is: Security at all costs.

It is no doubt lucky for man that life is so doubtful and unstable, for it prevents this born coward from winning the day. The pain and danger of life are on our side. Given pleasure and security, the born coward promptly goes to sleep. Only pain or inconvenience keep him on his feet. This is the reason behind the paradox of the indifference threshold.

Man's other self is geared entirely to purpose and evolution. He has glimpses of a joy that is beyond anything possible to the born coward: the ecstasy of power and freedom. He knows about the miseries and insecurities of human existence, about weakness and contingency.

But he does not believe in them, since he is certain that freedom is an absolute power. He knows that man is only subject to pain and misery insofar as he allows himself to be dominated by the coward, and that most human misfortune is another name for stupidity and self-pity. Consequently, he is inclined to suspect that even death may be a disguised form of suicide, and that human contingency will prove to be an illusion in the light of ultimate freedom. In short, he is totally the optimist and the adventurer; he cannot believe that human reason, powered by the human will to freedom, can ever encounter insurmountable obstacles.

This vision of man is not the outcome of romantic wishful thinking, but of the most rigorous phenomenological analysis.

Sartre and Heidegger are mistaken; it is not true that there is 'no exit' from the 'human dilemma.' There is a very clearly marked exit. Any man who can see this, and is capable of making the choice that the insight demands, has already taken the first step in a new phase of human evolution.

INDEX